International Labour and Employment Compliance Handbook

www.kluwerlawonline.com

Labour and Employment Compliance in Spain

International Bar Association

Labour and Employment Compliance in Spain

Twelfth Edition

Salvador del Rey

Ana Campos

This publication is part of the International Labour and Employment Compliance Handbook, available on www.kluwerlawonline.com

Editors: Salvador del Rey and Robert J. Mignin
Associate Editor: Juan Bonilla

the global voice of
the legal profession

Wolters Kluwer

Published by:
Kluwer Law International B.V.
PO Box 316
2400 AH Alphen aan den Rijn
The Netherlands
E-mail: lrs-sales@wolterskluwer.com
Website: www.wolterskluwer.com/en/solutions/kluwerlawinternational

Sold and distributed by:
Wolters Kluwer Legal & Regulatory U.S.
920 Links Avenue
Landisville, PA 17538
United States of America
E-mail: customer.service@wolterskluwer.com

ISBN 978-94-035-0039-3

e-Book: ISBN 978-94-035-0049-2
web-PDF: ISBN 978-94-035-0059-1

All listed titles are also available on lrus.wolterskluwer.com

1. Argentina: Julio César Stefanoni Zani & Enrique Alfredo Betemps, *Labour and Employment Compliance in Argentina, 12th edition*, 2024 (ISBN 978-94-035-4878-4)
2. Australia: John Tuck, Stephen Price, Rosemary Roach, Jack de Flamingh, Nicholas Ellery & Nick Le Mare, *Labour and Employment Compliance in Australia, 6th edition*, 2021 (ISBN 978-94-035-3914-0)
3. Belgium: Chris Van Olmen, *Labour and Employment Compliance in Belgium, 9th edition*, 2024 (ISBN 978-94-035-0089-8)
4. Brazil: Rodrigo Seizo Takano, Andrea Giamondo Massei & Murilo Caldeira Germiniani, *Labour and Employment Compliance in Brazil, 11th edition*, 2024 (ISBN 978-94-035-4938-5)
5. Canada: Kevin Coon, *Labour and Employment Compliance in Canada, 3rd edition*, 2023 (ISBN 978-90-411-9339-1)
6. Chile: Gerardo Otero A., María Dolores Echeverría F., María Ignacia Romero A., Juan Pablo Cortés R. & Javier Sabido, *Labour and Employment Compliance in Chile, 12th edition*, 2024 (ISBN 978-94-035-4968-2)
7. China: King & Wood Mallesons, *Labour and Employment Compliance in China, 6th edition*, 2021 (ISBN 978-94-035-3894-5)
8. France: Pascale Lagesse, *Labour and Employment Compliance in France, 11th edition*, 2023 (ISBN 978-94-035-2137-4)
9. Germany: Gerlind Wisskirchen & Martin Lützeler, *Labour and Employment Compliance in Germany, 11th edition*, 2023 (ISBN 978-94-035-2347-7)
10. India: Manishi Pathak, *Labour and Employment Compliance in India, 12th edition*, 2024 (ISBN 978-94-035-4908-8)
11. Ireland: Duncan Inverarity & Tríona Sugrue, *Labour and Employment Compliance in Ireland, 10th edition*, 2023 (ISBN 978-94-035-2227-2)
12. Israel: Pnina Broder-Manor & Ilan Winder, *Labour and Employment Compliance in Israel, 11th edition*, 2024 (ISBN 978-94-035-0099-7)
13. Italy: Angelo Zambelli, *Labour and Employment Compliance in Italy, 12th edition*, 2024 (ISBN 978-94-035-0009-6)
14. Japan: Yoshikazu Sugino, *Labour and Employment Compliance in Japan, 12th edition*, 2024 (ISBN 978-94-035-3158-8)
15. Republic of Korea: Sang Wook Cho, Soojung Lee, Christopher Mandel & Tae Eun Lee, *Labour and Employment Compliance in the Republic of Korea, 9th edition*, 2023 (ISBN 978-94-035-2167-1)
16. Mexico: Oscar De La Vega Gómez, *Labour and Employment Compliance in Mexico, 11th edition*, 2023 (ISBN 978-94-035-2377-4)
17. The Netherlands: Els de Wind & Cara Pronk, *Labour and Employment Compliance in the Netherlands, 5th edition*, 2022 (ISBN 978-94-035-1594-6)
18. Poland: Barbara Jóźwik, *Labour and Employment Compliance in Poland, 11th edition*, 2023 (ISBN 978-94-035-2407-8)
19. Russia: Anna-Stefaniya Chepik, *Labour and Employment Compliance in Russia*, 2013 (ISBN 978-90-411-4925-1)
20. Saudi Arabia: Sara Khoja & Sarit Thomas, *Labour and Employment Compliance in Saudi Arabia, 7th edition,* 2024 (ISBN 978-94-035-0129-1)

21. South Africa: Susan Stelzner†, Stuart Harrison, Brian Patterson & Zahida Ebrahim, *Labour and Employment Compliance in South Africa, 11th edition*, 2023 (ISBN 978-94-035-2257-9)
22. Spain: Salvador del Rey & Ana Campos, *Labour and Employment Compliance in Spain, 12th edition*, 2024 (978-94-035-0039-3)
23. Turkey: Elif Nur Çakır Vurgun, Gökhan Akçaalan, Özgür Kızıltan & Zeynep Adıyaman, *Labour and Employment Compliance in Turkey, 9th edition*, 2023 (ISBN 978-94-035-2287-6)
24. United Arab Emirates: Sara Khoja & Sarit Thomas, *Labour and Employment Compliance in the United Arab Emirates, 11th edition*, 2024 (ISBN 978-94-035-0159-8)
25. United Kingdom: Ed Mills, Ailie Murray, Anna West, Gareth Walls & Olivia Boyle, *Labour and Employment Compliance in The United Kingdom, 4th edition*, 2023 (ISBN 978-94-035-2317-0)
26. United States: Andrew J. Boling, Robert J. Mignin, Madeline F. Kelleher & David M. Serwer, *Labour and Employment Compliance in the United States, 8th edition*, 2023 (ISBN 978-94-035-1736-0)

International Bar Association
The Global Voice of the Legal Profession

The International Bar Association (IBA), established in 1947, is the world's leading organization of international legal practitioners, bar associations and law societies. The IBA influences the development of international law reform and shapes the future of the legal profession throughout the world. It has a membership of over 40,000 individual lawyers and almost 200 bar associations and law societies spanning all continents. It has considerable expertise in providing assistance to the global legal community.

Grouped into two divisions – the Legal Practice Division and the Public and Professional Interest Division – the IBA covers all practice areas and professional interests, providing members with access to leading experts and up-to-date information. Through the various committees of the divisions, the IBA enables an interchange of information and views among its members as to laws, practices and professional responsibilities relating to the practice of business law around the globe. Additionally, the IBA's high-quality publications and world-class conferences provide unrivalled professional development and network-building opportunities for international legal practitioners and professional associates.

The IBA's Bar Issues Commission provides an invaluable forum for IBA member organisations to discuss all matters relating to law at an international level.

The IBA's Human Rights Institute (IBAHRI) works across the Association, to promote, protect and enforce human rights under a just rule of law, and to preserve the independence of the judiciary and the legal profession worldwide.

Other institutions established by the IBA include the Southern Africa Litigation Centre and the International Legal Assistance Consortium.

Employment and Industrial Relations Law Committee

The aims of the committee are to develop and exchange knowledge of employment and industrial relations law and practice. Members support each other through the provision of innovative ideas and practical assistance on day-to-day issues. In addition, through its journal and through presentations, conferences, the committee ensures the dissemination of up-to-date law and practice in this highly important business area.

International Bar Association Global Employment Institute

The IBA Global Employment Institute (IBA GEI) was formed in early 2010 for the purpose of developing for multinationals and worldwide institutions a global and strategic approach to the key legal issues in the human resources and human capital fields.

Drawing on the resources and expertise of the IBA membership, the IBA GEI will provide a unique contribution in the field of employment, discrimination and immigration law, on a diverse range of global issues, to private and public organizations throughout the world. The IBA GEI is designed to enhance the management, performance and productivity of these organizations and help achieve best practice in their human capital and management functions from a strategic perspective.

The IBA GEI will become the leading voice and authority on global HR issues by virtue of having a number of the world's leading labour and employment practitioners in its ranks, and the support and resource of the world's largest association of international lawyers.

Further information

International Bar Association, 4th Floor, 10 St Bride Street, London EC4A 4AD, United Kingdom, Tel: +44 (0)20 7842 0090, Fax: +44 (0)20 7842 0091, E-mail: member@int-bar.org, www.ibanet.org

About the International Labour and Employment Compliance Handbook

From 1976 through 1988, the International Bar Association and Kluwer Law International published the groundbreaking International Handbook on Contracts of Employment. This Handbook provided one of the first global overviews of the law of the international employment relationship.

Since publishing the first edition, globalization of business has created an increased demand for knowledge of labor and employment laws throughout the world. Therefore, along with Kluwer, we decided to publish an updated Handbook which we have titled the International Labour and Employment Compliance Handbook.

This new Handbook was intended to be a practical guide by providing a general overview of key labor and employment issues in multiple jurisdictions. Each chapter was written so that it is easy to understand by lawyers and non-lawyers alike. Each country author has also followed a standard outline to assist readers in analysing employment issues in each country.

The first edition of this new Handbook included nineteen (19) different countries.

This Handbook would not have been possible without the help and assistance of many people. Most importantly, the individual country authors are all distinguished legal practitioners who spent considerable time drafting and revising their country reports to meet difficult deadlines. We thank each of them. Our friends at Kluwer, especially Ewa Szkatula, have done a wonderful job in keeping the editors and the authors on schedule. Finally, we want to also express our gratitude to Cuatrecasas, Gonçalves Pereira, and Baker & McKenzie LLP for their valuable assistance in the coordination and organization of this project. Our warmest thanks to each of them.

Because of the success of the Handbook,Wolters Kluwer Law & Business decided to publish each country report also as a separate book to give a choice in obtaining the information. We hope this new format will be a helpful and useful resource just like the Handbook. Both formats are available in print and online.

The Editors

Salvador del Rey Guanter
Robert J. Mignin

March 2013

Table of Contents

Spain

AUTHORS

Salvador del Rey

Salvador del Rey holds a PhD in Law with an extraordinary award from the University of Seville. He holds a Master of Science in Industrial and Labour Relations from Cornell University, NY. He was a visiting lecturer at the London School of Economics UK and at the Industrial and Labor Relations School at Cornell University. He was a practising attorney at Madrid and Barcelona Bar Associations and President of Honour of the Cuatrecasas Institute for Legal Strategy on Human Resources. Director of 'Encuentros La Ley-ESADE Labor Relations Forum'.

He is the author of thirty monographs and more than 200 articles and essays in joint books and in both national and foreign journals on labour law and industrial relations, new technologies and whistleblowing and a regular speaker at national and international meetings on his specialty.

He is an arbitrator at the Interconfederal Mediation and Arbitration Service and the Catalonia Employment Tribunal.

He was elected as one of the ten most prestigious labour lawyers worldwide according to the survey conducted by the directory Who's Who Management Labour; Employment Lawyers. He was distinguished also by this ranking as one of the five most prestigious lawyers in Europe. He was elected in 2023, 2022 and 2021 by Chambers Partners as a Senior Statesperson of work practice in Europe and also included in 2021 by *The Legal 500* in Employment in his Hall of Fame. He is recommended by other legal directories, such as Plc Which Lawyer, European Legal Experts or Best Lawyers.

He has been a member of several expert committees appointed by the Spanish Government to draft bills on different labour issues. He was

President of the Global Employment Institute of the IBA International Bar Association from 2010 to 2015, President of the Advisory Board of that Institute from 2016 to 2019 and Officer of the Legal Practice Division of the IBA from 2016 to 2019. From 2017 to 2019, he led the IBA Working Group, which prepared the 'Report on the Future of Work' for the ILO on the main global trends in the legal management of labour relations, especially under the impact of disruptive technologies.

Member of the Spanish Association of Labour Law (AEDTSS) and Founding Partner of the Spanish Forum of Labour Lawyers (FORELAB).

Ana Campos

Ana Campos received her Law degree and diploma in Business Management from Universidad Pontificia Comillas (ICADE), Spain, in 1997. In 2003, she obtained a Certificate in Human Resources Development from Harvard University Extension School. She has been an associate of the Labour and Employment Area of Cuatrecasas since 1998, providing ongoing advice on labour and social security issues to Spanish and multinational companies. Ms Campos is a member of the Knowledge and Innovation Area of the firm and a member of the Cuatrecasas Institute for Legal Strategy and Human Resources. She lectures on Labour and Employment Law and HR issues. She lectures on Employment Law at ISDE Law Business School. She is a member of the managing committee of the Employment Law section of the Madrid Bar Association.

ADDRESS

Cuatrecasas
Almagro, 9 / Av. Diagonal 191
Madrid 28010 / Barcelona 08018
Spain
Tel.: +34-93-2905446
+34-91-5247386
Fax: +34-93 312 53 94
E-mails: salvador.delrey@cuatrecasas.com
ana.campos@cuatrecasas.com
sergi.galvez@cuatrecasas.com
Web: www.cuatrecasas.com

Legal Compliance in Spain

1. THE LEGAL FRAMEWORK

In Spain, the laws and regulations that govern employer/employee relationships and working conditions are set forth in the EU Regulations and EU Directives of direct application, the Spanish Constitution, international treaties and International Labour Organization (ILO) Standards, the Workers' Statute, all national employment and social security laws and regulations, and the collective bargaining agreements.

It is relevant to explain briefly the territorial composition of Spain. The State is organized into towns, provinces and Autonomous Communities. There is a central government made up of the ministries, among which is the Ministry of Labour and Social Economy and the Ministry of Inclusion, Social Security and Migrations (*Ministerio de Trabajo y Economía Social, y el Ministerio de Inclusión, Seguridad Social y Migraciones*).

The State is divided territorially and politically into seventeen Autonomous Communities, which are geographical regions with political autonomy in many aspects. In relation to employment, the State has exclusive competence over the labour and employment legislation. However, the Constitution expressly allows for the transfer to the Autonomous Communities of the implementation and execution of labour legislation. Most Autonomous Communities have assumed these competences, and in consequence, the labour authorities that monitor compliance with the law are organisms of the Autonomous Communities.

1.1. Spanish Constitution

Section 14 of the Spanish Constitution prohibits discrimination based on birth, race, gender, religion, opinion or any other personal or social condition, such as age, sexual orientation, and affiliation with a political party or group.

Sections 15–29 of the Constitution contain a list of fundamental civil rights, which are protected by Spanish law and enforced by our judicial system. Along with such rights as the right to freedom of speech and the right to obtain effective judicial protection in courts and tribunals, the Spanish Constitution holds the freedom to belong or not belong to a union and the freedom to go on strike as fundamental civil rights.

The right to work is not included in this list, so it is not considered a fundamental civil right and in consequence, does not entail the same protection as the rights included in sections 14–29. It is included in section 35 of the Constitution, in the section titled 'Rights and Obligations of Citizens'.

1.2. The Workers' Statute and Other Labour Laws in Spain

The Workers' Statute has been refunded in *Real Decreto Legislativo 2/2015* on 23 October 2015. This law regulates individual employment relationships, including types of employment contracts, working time, terminations, collective representation rights, collective bargaining, and labour infractions.

Besides the Workers' Statute, there is a wide array of laws and regulations which govern employment relationships. The most relevant of these are the ones governing social security:[1] prevention of occupational hazards,[2] gender equality,[3] Temporary Employment Agencies (TEAs) law,[4] infringements and penalties of employment and social security obligations,[5] the law for the social jurisdiction,[6] trade union freedom law,[7] strike law[8] and the special regulations applicable to specific employment relationships,[9] such as top management relationships.

In the year 2023, relevant new legislation has been passed, the most outstanding from an employment relations perspective being:

---

1. *Real Decreto Legislativo 8/2015*, of 30 October, which sets forth the social security regulations.
2. *Ley 31/1995*, of 8 November, regarding the wide range of obligations relative to safety and health at work.
3. *Ley Orgánica 3/2007*, of 22 March, for the Equality Between Men and Women.
4. *Ley 14/1994,* of 1 June, of TEAs.
5. *Real Decreto Legislativo 5/2000*, of 4 August, which establishes the infractions and consequent penalties that may committed and applied to both employers and employees.
6. *Ley 36/2011*, of 10 October, which sets forth the different procedures for judicial employment conflicts.
7. *Ley Orgánica 11/1985*, of 2 August, of Trade Union Freedom.
8. *Real Decreto-Ley 17/1977*, of 4 March, of employment relations.
9. *Real Decreto 1382/1985*, of 1 August, which regulates the special employment relationship of top management personnel.

- Law 4/2023, for the full and effective equality of transgender people and for the guarantee of LGBTI rights.
- Royal Decree-Law 5/2023, which sets forth new regulations regarding work-family life balance.
- Directive (EU) 2023/970 to strengthen the application of the principle of equal pay for equal work or work of equal value between men and women through pay transparency and enforcement mechanisms.
- Besides, the European Parliament approved in March 2024 the Artificial Intelligence Act, the rules of which are aimed at regulating the use of Artificial Intelligence (AI) by manufacturers and providers of AI systems and by those responsible for the deployment of AI within the EU.

1.3. Collective Bargaining Agreements

Collective bargaining agreements are contracts negotiated between workers' representatives[10] and employers or employers' representatives to regulate working conditions in certain sectors or companies.

These agreements can only establish employment conditions that improve the ones established in the Workers' Statute; they cannot constitute a downgrading.[11] These agreements usually regulate working time, the working system (i.e., whether it is on a rotation system or not); remuneration, including yearly increases and benefits; a job description of each of the professional groups; vacation time; disciplinary procedures, including a description of disciplinary violations and the disciplinary measures the company may adopt. Agreements may also establish certain requirements for the engagement of new employees and impose on the company certain obligations regarding temporary employment contracts, such as a maximum percentage of temporary employees or a maximum duration for them.

Collective bargaining agreements have different scopes of application, depending on their functional and geographical scope. Employees are subject to a bargaining agreement, regardless of their affiliation with the bargaining trade union. Similarly, employers are bound by the agreement even if they (or their representatives) did not participate in negotiating the agreement.

There are national collective bargaining agreements for certain sectors (e.g., the Chemical Industry Agreement); provincial bargaining agreements (e.g., Madrid Collective Agreement for Offices and Firms); and company

10. Workers' representatives are the personnel delegates (in companies of less than fifty employees); members of the worker's committee elected by the workforce; and in some cases, trade union delegates (when there are sufficient members of the union in the company with members in the workers' committee).
11. As set forth in s. 85 of the Workers' Statute.

bargaining agreements (automotive companies or utility companies, for example), depending on the scope of the representation of the negotiating parties.

Collective agreements are temporary; the average term duration is three years.

They are published in the Official Bulletins, which, depending on the geographical scope of application, shall be the State's Official Bulletin (*Boletín Oficial del Estado,* BOE), the bulletin of each Autonomous Community, or the Official Bulletin for the province. They are legislation and one of the sources of the law for employment relationships.

Another source of regulations for employment relationships, as provided for in section 3 of the Worker's Statute, is the *individual employment contract*, which must necessarily respect all conditions established both in laws and regulations and in the applicable collective bargaining agreements.

1.4. Employee Benefits and Healthcare

In Spain, the social security system provides coverage for a series of contingencies, such as unemployment, temporary or permanent disability, retirement and death, and salary guarantee fund in case of a company's insolvency, widowhood and orphanhood. Its regulation is set forth in the Social Security General Law (*Real Decreto Legislativo 8/2015*, of 30 October, – *Ley General de Seguridad Social*). In order to pay for this coverage every employer and employee must contribute to the Social Security system for several contingencies. Contribution amounts are proportionate to the salary each employee receives (*see* section 10.6).

In Spain, the social security system provides universal healthcare coverage, as set forth in section 43 of the Constitution. Foreigners in irregular situations are also covered,[12] as established in the Foreigners' Policy Law (*Ley Orgánica 4/2000*, about rights and freedoms of foreign nationals in Spain and their social integration, amended by *Ley Orgánica 2/2009*, of 9 December).

12. Healthcare is provided for irregular foreigners in the following situations: minors (majority of age is attained at 18), pregnant women who give birth in Spain, foreigners registered in their local administrative offices (*Oficinas de Empadronamiento*). There are no requirements to be registered besides the passport.

2. CONTRACTS OF EMPLOYMENT

2.1. Overview

According to section 1 of the Workers' Statute, an employment relationship exists whenever a person renders services for another (whether an individual or a company) that assumes the risks and benefits of the business, who is called the 'employer', and the services are rendered within the scope of that person's managerial powers in exchange of a remuneration. The relationship exists regardless of whether there is a formal contract, either written or oral.

Individual employment contracts (also called *employment contracts* or *working contracts*) are used to establish specific rights and obligations for both employers and employees within the framework of Spanish labour laws and collective bargaining agreements. Any clause of the employment contract which should imply a downgrading of the regulations set forth in the law or the collective agreement will be considered null and void, and that condition agreed to shall be considered as not existing and may not be enforced. In these cases, the employment relationship will continue, and the condition to be enforced is the one set forth in the law or in the bargaining agreement.

Individual employment contracts usually define the position for which the employee has been hired, the date services are to start, remuneration, including variable compensation, working hours, vacation time, termination conditions, including prior-notice requirements, and the regulations applicable to the relationship. Certain agreements between the employer and the employee will not be considered valid unless they are included in the written working contract or an amendment thereto. For example, a requirement to work exclusively for the employer (an exclusivity clause) must be specified in the individual employment contract.

The parties are free to amend and modify the employment contract at any time during the employment relationship, always respecting the conditions established in the Workers' Statute and the bargaining agreements. Amendments and modifications must be approved by both parties.

The Workers' Statute or any applicable bargaining agreement shall apply by default to any conditions not specifically agreed upon in the employment contract.

Employment contracts are presumed to be of an indefinite length (versus temporary term) and by default considered to be full-time (versus part-time) with no trial period unless otherwise established.

2.2. Written Employment Contracts

An employer is not required by law to enter into a written individual employment contract with an employee; however, all employment for which there is no written employment signed between the parties is considered full-time (versus part-time) and will be indefinite (versus temporary).

An employer who wants to hire temporary or part-time work must enter into a written agreement. If the employment contract does not specify all its essential elements, the employer is obliged to inform the worker within the first two months of employment of the essential terms of the agreement.

These elements are as follows:

- Identification of the parties of the employment relationship.
- Date of commencement of the employment relationship. If the contract is temporary, the foreseeable duration of the relationship.
- Address of the company and the work centre where the employee renders his services.
- Employee's category or professional group in accordance with the collective bargaining agreement classification.
- Initial base salary and complements and payment frequency.
- Working hours and schedule.
- Amount of vacation time.
- Prior notice requirements in the event of termination for both parties.
- Applicable collective bargaining agreement.

Because of this obligation to inform employees in writing of these essential terms of their employment, most employers opt to enter into written employment contracts. There are also advantages to doing so, i.e., to obtain deductions on social security contributions.

The notification of these basic elements leaves the employer still unprotected if the employee takes action against him for issues related to the duration of employment (temporary or indefinite) and nature of the employment (part- or full-time).

On 20 June 2019, Directive 2019/1152 on transparent and predictable working conditions in the EU was published. It imposes obligations for the Member States to require employers to inform employees of the essential aspects of the employment relationship. This Directive includes a wide list of minimum information to be provided by employers, including, among others, that if the work pattern is entirely or mostly unpredictable, the employer must inform that the work schedule is variable, on the number of guaranteed paid hours and the remuneration of work performed over those guaranteed hours; the reference hours and days within which the worker may be required to work, and the minimum notice period to which the worker is entitled before the start of a work assignment and, where applicable, the deadline for cancellation. The transitional period for this Directive ended on 1 August 2022. The Spanish transposition is expected to be passed in the following months. Employers are also obliged to notify the public employment services of any new employment relationships within ten days of their initiation and provide the public employment services and the workers' representatives with a basic copy of the employment contract when the contracts should be in writing.

All employment not governed by a written employment contract is considered full-time and indefinite in duration. The Workers' Statute requires written employment contracts (sections 11–16 of the Workers' Statute) for all employees whose employment is not full-time or of an indefinite term. This includes all employees hired for apprenticeships, off-site working, part-time work, permanent non-continuous work, temporary employment, and employees hired in Spain to perform their services overseas for Spanish companies.

Employment contracts are presumed to be of an indefinite term.

In December 2021, the regulation of temporary recruitment was substantially modified, to limit its use, as Spain has one of the highest percentages of temporary employment contracts in the EU.

In consequence, since 30 March 2022, temporary recruitment is only allowed when it is necessary to cover situations of production overload and to replace another worker.

Employers are legally required to specify the reason for the temporary nature of contracts. They must indicate: (i) the grounds enabling the temporary recruitment, (ii) the specific circumstances justifying it, and (iii) the link between the reasons and the expected duration of the contract.

Temporary contracts grounded on production overload may be justified in two circumstances and will be subject to the following terms:

- Occasional and unexpected increases and fluctuations (i.e., not seasonal) in the company's normal activity, resulting in a temporary imbalance between the staff available and the staff required. In this case, contracts can last up to six months (or one year if so specified in the industry collective bargaining agreement). Fluctuations in activity include those resulting from annual vacations.
- Occasional, foreseeable situations that have a short, limited duration, in which case companies can enter into this type of contract with an unlimited number of employees for up to ninety (non-continuous) days in a calendar year.

Employers cannot use temporary contracts to execute contracting, subcontracting and administrative concessions that are part of the company's normal activity.

Employers may enter into replacement contracts on the following grounds:

- To replace an employee with the right to return to the same job, in which case the contract can start up to fifteen days before the beginning of the leave of the worker to be replaced.
- To cover the full working day of another employee whose hours have been reduced (for legal or contractual reasons).
- To temporarily cover a position during a selection or promotion process to find an indefinite employee, in which case the term of the temporary contract cannot exceed three months, or a shorter term under the collective agreement, and cannot be renewed for the same purpose once the temporary contract has expired.

All contracts are presumed to be indefinite, and the regulation sets out circumstances where they could become fixed-term contracts:

- Basic non-compliance with legal requirements.
- Failure to register the employee with Spanish Social Security after the probationary period.

Employees will also be considered indefinite workers if, within twenty-four months, they work under two or more subsequent temporary contracts for over eighteen months, including periods in which they are hired under a temporary-work agency, or if, during eighteen out of twenty-four months before, the employee's work position has been covered with other fixed-term contracts on production overload or hired through a temporary-work agency.

A breach of temporary recruitment regulations is considered an infringement for each employee affected by the breach, with penalties ranging between EUR 1,000 and EUR 10,000.

Temporary contracts lasting less than thirty days are subject to an additional social security contribution of EUR 26.6.

To channel flexible working arrangements, companies may use permanent seasonal contracts (*fijo-discontinuo*). This contract allows for the permanent hiring of employees who render their services in seasons or intermittently during specific, definite or indefinite periods.

Collective Bargaining agreements can govern how to call employees during inactivity for their reintegration into the activity and other details on the contracts. The call to permanent seasonal workers must be in writing or in a way that ensures that these workers are properly and timely notified of the exact conditions for their incorporation.

TEAs can enter into these contracts with their employees in order to lease them to other companies.

Companies that work as subcontractors must enter into permanent seasonal contracts with employees employed under a contractor agreement, whose periods of inactivity: (i) can only occur while they are waiting to be reassigned to a new outsourced job, and (ii) cannot extend beyond the maximum period provided under the sector-specific collective bargaining agreement or, failing that, three months, after which the company must take the contingency measures set out in the Workers' Statute.

2.3. Oral Contracts

Employment relationships can be entered into orally, except where a written contract is required by law, as explained in section 2.2 above. If there is a written contract and more favourable working conditions, have been established by oral contract, in the event of a conflict, the interested party will have to prove that the oral agreement took place after the execution of the employment contract. If there is no written contract at all, the orally established employment conditions will have to be proved if there is a conflict between the parties.

2.4. Remote Working

Remote working has been regulated by Law 10/2021, of 9 July. Remote working exists when 30% of the working day in a three-month reference period is carried out from home.

The main highlights of the remote working regulation are:

- Remote working does not enable to set of different working conditions and cannot be an obstacle to employees' rights.
- Remote working cannot be imposed; it is not in itself grounds for dismissal, and it is reversible for both parties.
- Remote working must be agreed in writing and agreement is required to modify its terms.
- Remote working cannot cost the worker money. Employers must provide the resources and tools necessary to carry out the work and the costs associated with the equipment.
- Remote workers are subject to the company's organization and control powers.

Collective bargaining agreements may complete the regulation on remote working on issues such as:

- The terms for exercising the right to cease remote working and return to on-site work (reversal).
- Provision and maintenance of the remote worker's resources by the company as required.
- Flexible hours for remote workers.
- Terms under which the company may establish conditions for using the provided IT resources, including personal use.
- Resources and measures for exercising the right to disconnect.
- Conditions to guarantee collective rights.

2.5 Employee Handbooks

Companies may establish any internal policies and procedures they deem convenient if they comply with the laws, the collective bargaining agreements and the employment contracts.

To disseminate these policies and procedures to employees, companies often distribute employee handbooks. These may be general handbooks covering day-to-day matters such as employee travel expenditures, reimbursement procedures and policies, or vacation time. It is now quite frequent for companies to introduce codes of conduct for the prevention of mobbing and with respect to employees' use of new technologies. Both the employer and the employees are bound by rules, policies and procedures set forth in the handbooks.

Protocols and policies are required to comply with laws on health and safety, gender equality and prevention of sexual harassment, sexual violence, information systems, use of digital devices, working time register, right to disconnect and remote working.[13]

2.6. Job Descriptions

Job descriptions include the relevant aspects of the job and may not contain discriminatory statements or requirements in compliance with section 14 of the Spanish Constitution. A collective bargaining agreement usually includes a job description of all the professional categories in the industry or company, depending on its scope of application. Such agreements establish the salary for each professional category.

Job descriptions are relevant to place employees in the correct professional category in accordance with the functions effectively carried out by them. Employees' professional category cannot be unilaterally

13. *Ley 31/1995*, of 8 November, for the Prevention of Occupational Hazards and *Ley Orgánica de Igualdad 3/2007*, of 22 March, for the equality of men and women.

modified by the employer; that is, an employee cannot be assigned to carry out functions in a different professional category without agreeing to it, as it would constitute functional mobility, which must follow the procedure established in section 39 of the Workers' Statute.

Section 39 allows for functional mobility within the ranges of the employee's qualifications (academics or professional) required for the position and respects the employee's dignity. If the mobility is between different professional categories, it may be carried out only when objective technical or operational causes concur, and for the shortest possible time, and if the mobility should imply inferior functions, the reasons must also be urgent and peremptory.

If an employee should carry out superior functions than the ones initially agreed to for a period of six months within a year or eight months within two years, the employee will be entitled to claim the promotion and the corresponding salary raise.

2.7. Offer Letters

Offer letters are documents in which a company states the decision to enter into an employment contract and the terms that it has offered. The offer is not binding until it is formalized in the employment contract.

If the prospective employee accepts the offer letter, and the company backs out before the employment contract is signed or comes into force, the company may be liable for damage claims from the prospective employee if he or she adopted measures in order to start working in the offered position (such as giving notice at a previous job or relocating).

2.8. Checklist of Do's and Don'ts

– It is advisable to put all employment contracts in writing as it reduces the risks in case of conflict and conflicts themselves and facilitates paperwork and management of human resources.
– Avoid misusing temporary employment contracts, for example, using them when the circumstances justifying the temporary term do not exist, because the consequences usually are more costly than the severance pay for an indefinite-term contract.
– Verify the regulation established in the applicable collective bargaining agreement since they are a source of regulation.

3. RECRUITING, INTERVIEWING, SCREENING AND HIRING EMPLOYEES

3.1. Overview

Under Spanish law, the employer has a duty to protect the employee as a person, and such protection is carried out through the protection of the employee's privacy and dignity, established in the privacy right (section 4.2) of the Workers' Statute.

There are no specific regulations under Spanish law indicating which and how questions shall be asked in the recruiting process so as not to breach the candidates' privacy rights. Apart from the rulings by the EU Directives and the conventions of the ILO signed by Spain, most of the references to the rights of the candidates in the recruiting process are contained in the following legal provisions:

- Section 14 of the Spanish Constitution prohibits discrimination based on birth, race, gender, political or religious beliefs, or due to any other personal or social condition or circumstance.
- Section 18 of the Spanish Constitution guarantees the citizens' rights to personal honour and privacy for themselves and their families.
- Section 4 of the Workers' Statute prohibits any kind of positive or negative discrimination in the access to employment or working conditions on the basis of gender, marital status, age, race or ethnic origin, social status, religious or political beliefs, sexual orientation, union affiliation or language.
- Section 17 of the Workers' Statute declares void of any decision deemed discriminatory.
- Section 5 of the Gender Equality Law declares the right for equal treatment in the access to work.
- Section 3 of the Law for Equal Treatment and Non-discrimination prohibits discrimination in access to employment based on illness, health condition, serological status and genetic predisposition to pathologies and disorders, as well as gender expression, language, and socioeconomic status.

3.2. Recruiting

Case law issued by the Constitutional Court establishes that the principles of non-discrimination also apply to recruitment processes and the limitation to attempts against individual privacy rights (Judgment of 2 March 1999).

The right of the employer to request information from the candidate may depend, then, on the position to be covered and the need for candidates with specific qualifications or characteristics. Thus, unless there is a direct and lawful connection with the employment position to be covered and the tasks to be developed, the employer cannot request any information on the candidates' private lives. In any event, it is a common practice in Spain that employers ask most questions; the candidate has the option not to answer those that are not relevant to the job or intrude in his/her privacy sphere.

The Workers' Statute obligates employers to inform part-time and/or temporary employees of job openings in the company before looking for personnel outside the company, either by posting a public announcement in a visible place in the company or by any other way established in the collective agreement.

According to Law 3/2007, for Gender Equality, companies must ensure that both men and women have an equal chance to be recruited. This Law establishes that companies have to introduce and implement an Equality Plan consisting of a coordinated set of measures to ensure that men and women receive equal treatment and opportunity, specifically, equal access to employment. With respect to equal access to employment, the Equality Plan may require that the company's job advertisements are gender-neutral or that the company publicizes its commitment to gender-neutral policies. The design and implementation of these plans require a prior audit of equality in the company.

3.3. Employment Applications

In Spain, personal data of individuals contained in employment applications are specially protected because of Regulation (EU) 2016/679 on the protection of natural persons with regard to the processing of personal data and on the free movement of such data, and repealing Directive 95/46/EC (General Data Protection Regulation, GDPR). The corresponding law is Organic Law 3/2018 on the Protection of Personal Data and Guarantee of Digital Rights (Ley Orgáncia de Protección de Datos y Garantía de Derechos Digitales, LOPDGDD), and its purpose is to ensure the security and privacy of the handling of private data of individuals.

The mentioned GDPR enabled Member States to lay down specific rules in order to ensure the protection of personal data in the employment field. Accordingly, with respect to employment applications, the LOPDGDD considers the information contained in an application for employment as personal data (which is defined in the law as any information relative to identified or identifiable individual people), which cannot be used for any other purpose except for the use they were provided for. An employer may not, for example, send the applicant's filled-out application to another company to be used in that company's recruiting process. Neither can an employer use the applicant's address for its own publicity or promotional mailings. The candidate must be informed of how the information is going to be used. The law also requires that all documents relating to unsuccessful applicants must be destroyed at the end of the recruiting process to avoid potential mistreatment of personal data or third-party access to such data.

3.4. Pre-employment Enquiries

Law 15/2022, for equal treatment and non-discrimination, in force since 14 July 2022, forbids employers from asking job applicants about their health condition.

Besides, pre-employment enquiries must respect the fundamental civil rights guaranteed by the Constitution.

For example, a pre-employment enquiry cannot violate the prospective employee's right to privacy. Thus, an employer cannot investigate prospective employees' private life (family status, lifestyle, affiliations, preferences, etc.).

3.5. Pre-employment Tests and Examinations

Companies are allowed to carry out all the tests and examinations needed to assess performance for the jobs for which the recruiting process is being carried out.

Testing for job skills is becoming frequent in recruiting procedures in Spain. In most cases, practical tests and exams are permitted during the recruiting process. However, all results obtained must be kept confidential and can be only used if they are relevant to the position offered to the candidate.

3.6. Background, Reference and Credit Checks

Spanish law does not allow an employer to do credit checks on applicants as part of the recruiting process, deeming such investigation to be an illegal invasion of the candidate's private life.

However, a prospective employee may be asked to supply references from past employers, and this is done frequently, especially in sectors where the academic education received is not so relevant (i.e., for lower-level positions which do not require academic degrees).

It is not against the law to request information from a former or current employer. The former or current employer is not obliged to provide such information, but if they are willing to do so in an informal way, there is no legal issue. However, the handing over of written information from former or current employers (especially if personal data or personal assessments are included) may require the prior consent of the candidate because the Law for Personal Data Protection would apply.

3.7. Interviewing

There is no specific regulation on interviewing for a job position, except for the necessary respect for fundamental civil rights.

Although not specifically established in the law, employers should not ask about the prospective employee's intention to start a family, political views, or religious beliefs, and, moreover, employees are not obliged to answer such questions. If such questions are asked, the candidate has a right to report it to the Labour and Social Security Inspectorate. However, it is difficult to find proof that the employee was not hired for those reasons or even for those questions being asked.

3.8. Hiring Procedures

When an employer decides to hire a candidate, the conditions of employment must be clearly set forth: working hours, schedule and remuneration in compliance with the applicable collective agreement. Any other special provisions (prior-notice requirements, non-compete, exclusivity, variable compensation, etc.) must be specified in the written employment contract. The contract may be amended at any time by mutual agreement between the parties.

3.9. Fines and Penalties

- Discriminatory recruiting and hiring practices constitute a very serious infraction, subject to sanctions ranging from EUR 7,501 to EUR 225,018.[14]
- Any violation of the employee's right to privacy is a very serious infraction of the employer's obligations, is a violation of employment laws and is subject to a sanction ranging from EUR 7,501 to EUR 225,018.

14. *Real Decreto Legislativo 5/2000*, of 4 August, of infractions and penalties in labour relations.

- Failure to inform part-time and/or temporary employees of the vacancies existing in the company constitutes a minor infraction, which may be fined from EUR 70 to EUR 750.
- Misuse of temporary employment contracts constitutes a serious infraction, with a fine ranging from EUR 1,000 to EUR 10,000 per affected employee.

3.10. Checklist of Do's and Don'ts

- Do not ask in the process, recruiting materials or job applications any questions unrelated to the job or position, as, among others, if they owe money, their criminal background or drug consumption, if they are actively involved in political or civic activities or family status.
- Treat the information in employment applications as confidential and protect it from third-party access.
- Be straightforward during the recruiting process to avoid misunderstanding and false expectations.
- If signing an employment contract, establish that it has precedence over any verbal discussion.

4. MANAGING EMPLOYEE PERFORMANCE/CONDUCT

4.1. Overview

In the employment relationship, employees are subject to employers' managerial power, which means that it is the employer's responsibility and prerogative to organize the work and issue orders. Employers are entitled to use disciplinary measures (*see* section 4.4) if employees fail to comply with their obligations.

The general obligations of employees to their employers are set forth in section 5 of the Workers' Statute. Spanish courts have interpreted and extended this list, considering the circumstances in each case.

The Workers' Statute provides that employees 'have the following basic obligations':

- Diligently and in good faith perform the duties of their position.
- Observe health and safety rules in the workplace.
- Carry out the employer's reasonable and pertinent orders and instructions.
- Not compete against the employer's activity, as established by the law.[15]

---

15. As set forth in s. 21 of the Worker's Statute (obligation of non-concurring against the employer) and s. 54, competition against the employer is one of the valid causes for disciplinary termination.

- Contribute to an increase in the company's productivity.
- And any other obligations set forth in the employment contract.

4.2. Coaching and Counselling

Under Spanish law, companies are not obliged to provide counselling or coaching to employees, although some larger companies include these services in their human resources policies and for performance evaluation purposes. Typically, such coaching involves professional training.

4.3. Written Evaluations

Some companies establish a system for evaluating performance to determine whether employees deserve a promotion or a bonus.

4.4. Warnings and Suspensions

Under the Workers' Statute, serious employee misconduct justifies termination of the employment contract. How serious the conduct must be to justify the termination is largely within the judge's discretion. The judge will consider all the circumstances of the case.

Collective bargaining agreements establish both the misconduct (faults) and the disciplinary measures that may be applied to minor infringements of the employee's obligations that are not serious enough to justify termination.

These disciplinary measures usually range from oral warnings to suspension of employment and pay for a certain period and even termination of the employment contract. Certain disciplinary measures, such as reducing vacation time or pecuniary fines, are not allowed.[16] Disciplinary measures adopted by the company will be considered null if they are discriminatory.

Some collective agreements establish a formal procedure for the imposing of disciplinary measures. Failure to follow it results in the disciplinary measures being invalid. These procedures require that the employee must be clearly informed in writing of his or her alleged misconduct and the disciplinary action that may be taken. Usually, the employee who is to be disciplined is then heard by the company in a hearing at which workers' representatives could also present to determine whether any measure is to be adopted and which one. The decision of whether or not to sanction belongs to the company. Workers' representatives may be heard, but their opinion is not binding on the company.

16. Section 58.3 of the Workers' Statute.

Imposing disciplinary measures on workers' representatives always requires a formal procedure.

Any disciplinary procedure and measures imposed must be recorded in the employee's file. When misconduct occurs several times within a certain period, it is frequently considered an aggravation of the posterior misconduct as a recurrence of infringement.

The employee's misconduct may only be disciplined within a certain time frame (a statute of limitations) after it has occurred or after the employer had knowledge of the misconduct. The time limits are as follows:

- Minor misconduct: ten days.
- Serious misconduct: twenty days.
- Very serious misconduct: sixty days.

Each collective bargaining agreement establishes its own graduation of misconduct.

Once a disciplinary measure has been adopted, the employee is entitled to judicially contest its fairness. The industrial courts have jurisdiction over employment and labour relationships.

4.5. Checklist of Do's and Don'ts

- Be very clear about the company's policy on disciplinary measures. When determining whether a disciplinary measure was justified, the court will, for example, take into consideration whether the disciplinary system established in the collective bargaining agreement was strictly applied or whether the company was somewhat lenient.
- Avoid adopting disciplinary measures that may be considered discriminatory, for example, disciplining a woman for missing working time because of her doctors' appointments during pregnancy.
- Fully document and justify all disciplinary measures to be adopted.
- Strictly follow the procedure for disciplinary measures in the applicable collective agreement.
- Keep to the legally established time frame since the notification of the measure requires the consignation of the dates of the misdemeanour and also when the company became aware of it.

5. TERMINATION OF EMPLOYEES FOR PERFORMANCE OR DISCIPLINARY REASONS

5.1. Overview

Under Spanish law, termination of employment must be for cause, which may be a disciplinary reason as set forth in section 54 of the Workers'

Statute. Employment may be terminated for performance and disciplinary reasons without severance pay if the misconduct of the employee is sufficiently serious as to justify the termination with no right to severance compensation.

The following conduct is considered to be a breach of contract (i.e., a breach of the obligations of the employment relationship, whether or not there is a written contract) as set forth in section 54 of the Workers' Statute. Depending on the seriousness of the conduct in each case, it may justify termination:

- Repeated unjustified absences from work or unpunctuality.
- Indiscipline and disobedience in the employee's performance of duties.
- Verbal or physical offences against the employer or other company employees or their families.
- Breach of contractual good faith and abuse of trust, for example, using the company's credit card to pay for personal expenses.
- Voluntary and continuous decrease in established performance standards.
- Common drunkenness or drug addiction when it negatively affects the employee's work.
- Harassment of the employer or of any persons working in the company based on race or ethnicity, religious or personal convictions, disabilities, age, or sexual orientation, including sexual and gender harassment.

Notification of termination must be in writing and must specify the reasons for the termination in as much detail as possible, including a description of the employees' misconduct, the dates on which it happened, the reasons the employer considers it serious enough to justify termination and a citation of the regulation(s) supporting the termination.

If sufficiently serious, any of the above-mentioned behaviours may justify the termination without severance pay.

Employees terminated for disciplinary reasons usually challenge the termination before the industrial courts unless the employer acknowledges the unfairness of the termination, meaning there is no sufficient cause for it, and in consequence, the employee is entitled to severance compensation. When challenged, decisions vary greatly in the different courts, as the judges take into account all the circumstances in each case and decide on the seriousness of the misconduct and the fairness of the dismissal. It falls on employers to prove the misconduct and its seriousness.

The employment law general principle *in dubio pro operario* ('in doubt for the operator or worker') must be considered. This principle means that if the court has any doubt about the evidence of a conflict between an employer and an employee, it must rule in favour of the employee. Thus, judges do not declare the fairness of dismissal unless the employer has proved the seriousness of the employees' misconduct.

If an employee does not challenge the termination, it is taken to mean that the employee has accepted it, and thus there is no severance pay.

5.2. Separation/Severance Pay

Terminations based on disciplinary grounds may be considered fair, unfair or null and void.

5.2.1. Fair Termination

If the employee challenges the termination decision and the judge declares it fair (because the employee's misconduct is sufficiently serious), the employee will not be entitled to severance pay. In this case, the employee is only entitled to all salary accrued up to the date of termination and payment for accrued vacation leave.

5.2.2. Unfair Termination

The termination shall be declared unfair if there is no cause or if the alleged cause is not sufficiently serious to justify the dismissal. In such cases, the required severance pay is thirty-three days' salary per year worked, up to a maximum of twenty-four monthly instalments. This is the severance compensation in force since 2012, formerly, the severance compensation for unfair termination was forty-five calendar days' salary per year of service up to a maximum of forty-two monthly instalments.

For employment relationships before the effective date of Royal Decree-Law on urgent measures regarding the labour market (12 February 2012), severance payment shall amount to forty-five calendar days' salary per year of service for the time worked before the Royal Decree-Law became effective, and thirty-three calendar days' salary per year of service for the time worked after the Royal Decree-Law became effective. If the compensation accrued till 12 February 2012 is over 720 calendar days (twenty-four monthly instalments), the number of days accrued will be the maximum compensation. The severance compensation will never be over forty-two monthly instalments.

If the termination is declared unfair, or the employer acknowledges its unfairness, the employer may choose between: (i) reinstating the employee, in which case the employee would be entitled to all back pay from the date of termination, that is, all back salary from the date of termination until the date of the court's decision and (ii) terminating the employee with legal compensation.

The legal severance pay is tax-exempt up to a maximum of EUR 180,000, although it is required to acknowledge the unfairness of the termination and the amount of the compensation at the mediation and conciliation office[17] or before the judge.

All remuneration the employee has received, both in cash and in kind, except reimbursement for work-related expenses, must be considered as the base of calculation of the severance compensation.

The following is an example of a severance compensation calculation: An employee with a yearly salary of EUR 60,000 and seniority of 30 May 2011 is unfairly terminated on 30 May 2024.

It is necessary to know the daily salary (yearly salary/365):

- EUR 60,000/365 = EUR 164.38 per day.
- Severance compensation.
- Seniority until February 2012 [3.75] × EUR 164.38 × 45 days salary = EUR 5,547.95 severance pay.
- Seniority from 12 February 2012 till termination date (30 May 2024) × EUR 164.38 × 33 days salary = EUR 66,904.11 severance pay.
- Total severance pay = EUR 72.452.05.
- Forty-two monthly instalments limit (EUR 60,000/12 = EUR 5,000) × 42 = EUR 210,000.
- Twenty-four monthly instalments limit (EUR 60,000/12 = 5,000) × 24 = 120,000.

With respect to unfair dismissals, workers' representatives are specially protected. If their dismissal is unfair, the representative, instead of the employer, is entitled to choose between termination and reinstatement under the terms and conditions stated above. The representative is entitled to back pay regardless of his choice between termination and reinstatement. Also, an internal company procedure must be followed for their disciplinary dismissal before it can take place, in which there has to be a formal hearing of the representative in the presence of other workers' representatives.

5.2.3. Null and Void Termination

If the court finds that the dismissal was based on discriminatory reasons, the termination shall be declared null and void, and the employer will be obliged

17. Termination procedures require before going to court a compulsory attempt at conciliation, first at the mediation and conciliation office and on second instance before the judge. The mediation and conciliation office is an administrative agency existing in each Autonomous Community.

to reinstate the employee in his or her former position with all back pay. In some cases, the company may also be ordered to pay moral damages.

There are some terminations which are automatically null and void even though there are no discriminatory grounds unless the employer is able to prove the employee committed a serious infringement of the employment contract which justified termination or that there were sufficient objective reasons for termination. That is, terminations in these cases cannot be considered unfair (which would entail the termination of the contract with severance pay); they are either fair – that is, there is cause for termination – or they are null and void.

This protection is applicable to employees whose employment contracts are suspended because of: (i) maternity, (ii) health risk during the pregnancy period or during the breastfeeding period, (iii) sickness due to pregnancy, delivery or natural breastfeeding period, (iv) adoption or fostering, or (v) during the paternity leave.

This protection also applies to pregnant employees[18] between the start of the pregnancy and the suspension of their employment contract for maternity leave and to employees who have suspended their employment contract for maternity, paternity, adoption or fostering leaves for twelve months after the birth, adoption or fostering day. This protection also applies to employees who are enjoying a reduction in their daily working time because of breastfeeding or the birth of premature children. This applies even if the child is being bottle-fed, and it applies to both men and women.

It is also null and void to terminate employees who have a reduction[19] in their working time because they are the primary caregiver and legal guardian of a child twelve years old or younger or are the primary caregiver of a family member with a serious disability which renders him or her unable to take care of him/herself. Employees victims of domestic violence who are enjoying a reduction in their working time are also protected.

The declaration of nullity implies the reinstatement of the employee and payment of all accrued salaries. However, in practice, it is often the case that reinstatement in these circumstances is not desirable to either the employee or the employer, and so agreements on severance compensation may be negotiated with these specially protected employees to terminate their employment contract. In such cases, the amount usually agreed on is at least the same as for unfair terminations.

Upon termination of employment for any reason, employers must provide employees with the termination paperwork, which is namely, the document

18. The Constitutional Court on 21 Jul. 2008 (Decision 92/2008) decided that the termination of a pregnant employee was null and void regardless of the knowledge by the company of the pregnancy.

19. This working time reduction may range from one-eighth of the working time to a maximum of half of the working time (s. 37.5 of the Workers' Statute). During the COVID-19 crisis this reduction can reach 100% of the working time.

detailing the accrued salaries and vacation time and their payment, a tax certificate and a social security certificate, which the employee will need in order to claim and receive unemployment compensation.

5.3. Fines and Penalties

Failure to perform the administrative requirements of the termination paperwork of terminated employees is a serious infraction on the part of the employer, which may be fined from EUR 751 to EUR 7,500.[20]

5.4. Checklist of Do's and Don'ts

- Verify the employee's status, such as pregnancy, maternity or paternity leave, part-time working hours (to care for young children) and victims of domestic violence.
- Verify the employee's salary for severance pay purposes, as any mistakes on this matter may lead to litigation and higher costs.
- Verify whether the collective bargaining agreement establishes a specific procedure to be followed when terminating employees on disciplinary grounds.
- Specify in the termination letter the reasons for the dismissal; be as descriptive as possible and include all the necessary details.

6. LAYOFFS, REDUCTIONS IN WORKFORCE, AND/OR REDUNDANCIES AS A RESULT OF JOB ELIMINATIONS OR OTHER RESTRUCTURING

6.1. Overview

Layoffs, reductions in workforce and/or redundancies and other restructuring are subject to the Workers' Statute (sections 51 and 52).

Individual layoffs must be based on the following objective reasons (section 52 of the Workers' Statute):

- Ineptitude on the part of the employee known or arising after the rendering of services for the company has begun. If this ineptitude is known to the company during the trial period, it may not be alleged afterwards to justify the termination.

20. *Real Decreto Legislativo 5/2000*, of 4 August, of infractions and penalties in labour relations.

- Lack of adaptation to technical modifications of the job position, as long as the changes are reasonable and two months since the introduction of the modifications have passed. In these cases, the employer must have offered the employee an adaptation course.
- When there is a proven necessity of amortization of job positions because of reasons of an economic, technical, productive or operational nature.

Amortizations of job positions based on economic, technical, productive, or operational reasons are frequently used. They are applicable to either *collective* (section 51 of the Workers' Statute) or *individual* (section 52 of the Workers' Statute) layoffs, depending on the number of employees affected by the terminations (*see* section 6.2).

Regarding economic grounds, under law, there must be a negative economic situation, current or foreseen; 'a persistent decrease in income or sales' is evidence of such situation. The law considers a decrease in income or sales to be persistent if it takes place during three consecutive quarters compared to the same quarter of the previous year.

As for productive, technical, and organizational grounds, the law no longer requires companies to prove the reasonability of the dismissal as a measure to prevent companies' negative performances. These reasons are defined as follows:

- *Technical*: changes, among others, on the production means or tools.
- *Organizational*: changes, among others, in the work systems or methods or in the production organization.
- *Productive*: changes, among others, in demand for products or services that the company wants to sell in the market.

6.2. Reductions in Force/Layoffs/Job Eliminations

6.2.1. Collective Versus Individual Reductions in the Workforce

The reduction in workforce is collective if, within a ninety-day period, it affects:

- At least ten employees in a company of less than 100 employees.
- At least 10% of the employees in companies with between 100 and 300 employees.
- At least thirty employees in companies with three hundred or more employees.

According to case law, the reference for the terminations is not only the company but the work centre, when the work centre has at least twenty employees.

If the number of employees affected is below these thresholds, the termination will have to be carried out following the procedure for individual layoffs.

6.2.2. Procedure

In the case of an *individual termination*, the employee must be given fifteen days prior written notice *fully explaining* the reasons for the termination. During this period, the employee is entitled to six hours of paid leave per week to look for another job.

Simultaneously with the written notice, the employer must give the employee the legal severance pay equal to twenty days' salary per year worked,[21] up to a maximum of twelve monthly instalments. If this severance compensation requirement is not complied with, the termination is unfair.

Nevertheless, if the termination is based on economic reasons that justify not paying the compensation at that time, and the employer explains the situation in the termination letter, the failure to pay the severance compensation does not void the termination. This lack of payment does not waive the right of the employee to receive the compensation when the termination should be effective. In other words, under these circumstances, the payment of the severance compensation can be deferred.

If the employer fails to comply with the fifteen-day prior notice requirement, the employee is entitled to payment of each omitted day of prior notice.

For *collective dismissals,*[22] the law requires the employer to negotiate the restructuring with the workers' representatives with the intention of reaching an agreement. The negotiation period must last no more than thirty[23] days in companies with more than fifty employees and fifteen days in companies with fewer employees.

Prior to the formal beginning of the negotiation period, the employer must notify the employees of its intention to initiate a collective dismissal for the affected employees to designate their representatives during the negotiation. This designation must take place within either seven or fifteen days, depending on whether there are legal representatives in the affected work centres. The designated representatives shall constitute a representatives committee made up of either the trade unions, the legal representatives of the employees, or an ad hoc committee.

21. This is the severance compensation for fair termination based on objective reasons, if the termination is unfair, the compensation is forty-five/thirty-three days' salary per year worked.
22. Section 51 of the Workers' Statute.
23. Although the parties may agree to negotiate for a longer period, if an agreement is envisaged.

The lack of designation within the legal period shall not prevent the continuation of the process.

Consequently, the collective dismissal procedure will commence formally and officially with an official communication to the representatives committee, which marks the initiation of the negotiation period. This notification must contain the following information:

- The reasons for the collective redundancy.
- The number and professional group of employees affected by the termination.
- The criteria used to decide which employees are to be affected.
- The number and professional groups of the employees of the company in the previous year.
- The period over which the redundancies will be carried out must also be informed.

The Labour Authority must receive a copy of this document together with all the rest of the information.

The employer, at the same time as notifying the initiation of the procedure, must provide the workers' representatives with the documentation justifying and proving the reasons for the collective dismissal.

This documentation includes the following:

(a) If the cause is *economic*, the documentation to be provided by the company must include a report in which the company's economic situation is proved, supported by any documents the employer may consider relevant. The following are compulsory:
   - Audited financial and patrimonial statements for the previous two years relating to the company's development and situation.
   - If the alleged economic negative situation is foreseen, the employer must also provide the criteria used for such estimation. Also, a report on the volume and transitional or definitive nature of the situation, based on annual accounts, sector data, market evolution and the position of the company.
   - If the economic situation is based on a persistent decrease in income or sales, the employer must also provide the tax and accounting documents proving such decrease, corresponding to at least three-quarters prior to the collective termination, as well as for the three same quarters of the previous year.
   - If the company belongs to a group of companies, it must provide evidence of the economic situation with documents of the group of companies obliged to present consolidated accounts. This obligation refers to the consolidated annual accounts and

management report of the controlling company of the group corresponding to the last two financial years.
- If there is no obligation to present consolidated accounts, the company seeking to carry out the terminations must submit, in addition to its own economic documentation, that of the other companies of the group with registered address in Spain, have the same activity as the applicant company or belong to the same sector of activity and have debtor or creditor balances with the applicant company.

(b) If the cause is *technical, operational, or productive*, the plans, projects and technical reports justifying the cause, including the measures to be adopted and the expected consequences for the company's future viability.

Besides this documentation, the employer must present a *memorandum* that fully explains all the circumstances of the company which determine the necessity of downsizing.

The negotiation period is the pivotal centre of the collective termination procedure. Its purpose is to attempt to find alternatives to avoid or reduce the terminations and to attenuate their consequences by establishing accompanying social measures such as relocations, training or retraining to improve employability. Both parties must negotiate in good faith. Minutes of each meeting between the parties must be drafted and signed by all, stating the positions of each, as well as the offers and counteroffers.

The negotiation period and the information provided to the workers' representatives have become the core of the collective procedure, without which it may be declared null and void. The judgments on the collective terminations carried out since the labour reform have stressed the importance of there being a real negotiation between the parties, rejecting unjustified immovable positions by the parties, and requiring proposals and counterproposals from both parties. It is not compulsory to give in to employees' proposals, but refusals must be reasoned and justifiable.

If the collective termination affects more than fifty employees, it is compulsory to offer an *outplacement plan* by way of external outplacement companies. This plan must be offered at the beginning of the bargaining period (although its content may vary during the bargaining) and shall be designed for a minimum period of six months, including measures of:

- intermediation activities (matching employment offers with the affected employees);
- professional training and guidance;
- personalized attention to the affected workers; and
- active job search.

The Labour Authority must require the Labour and Social Security Inspectorate to report on the notification of the initiation of the negotiation period, as well as on the development of such period.

6.2.3. Termination of the Procedure

If the parties reach an agreement during the negotiation period, the employer shall notify the Labour Authority and carry out the terminations in accordance with the agreement. The negotiating parties can agree to any severance pay, with a minimum of twenty days' salary per year worked up to a maximum of twelve monthly payments.

If an agreement has not been reached after the negotiation period with the employees' legal representatives, the company may decide to enforce the collective redundancies anyway. It is compulsory to notify its decision to the workers' representatives. The employer must then notify the terminations individually, with the same formal requirements as for individual redundancies, and at least thirty days must have elapsed since the beginning of the negotiation period and the effective date of termination.

The final decision must be notified within fifteen days of the end of the negotiation period.

This signifies, among other things, that the company must proceed to: (i) communicate in writing individually to the affected employees the objective grounds justifying the termination of their employment contract; (ii) simultaneously pay the compensation of twenty days per year of service with a limit of twelve monthly payments; and, (iii) grant a minimum of fifteen days' advance notice. In addition, and in all cases, it is laid down that the minimum period between the opening date of the consultation period to the labour relations authorities and the effective date of the termination may not be less than thirty days.

The decision adopted by the employer may be challenged before the courts. This objection will normally be collective – by way of the workers' legal representatives – in the event of the consultation period finishing without agreement. Competence for ruling on these collective processes will correspond to the Labour Relations Chambers of the High Court of Justice (*Tribunal Superior de Justicia*) or the National Court (*Audiencia Nacional*), depending on the geographical scope of the conflict.

However, even when an agreement is reached with the workers' legal representatives, terminations of employment contracts within the framework of a collective redundancy procedure can also be contested individually by each employee.

The court shall declare the terminations legally adjusted, unadjusted, or null and void. Failure to provide the required information or to effectively negotiate shall render the procedure null and void.

The decisions by the labour courts reveal that the judges are being very strict on the accomplishment by the companies of: (i) the formalities indicated by the law (the provision of all documents evidencing the need for the terminations), (ii) the need to clearly identify the affectation criteria for the employees that will be made redundant, and (iii) that the consultation and bargaining period has taken place and negotiations were done in good faith.

6.2.4. Contribution to the Public Treasury

Additional Disposition 16 of Law 27/2011[24] on Social Security sets the obligation of the companies to afford contributions to the National Treasury when carrying out collective redundancies, including employees of 50 or more years of age when the following circumstances occur:

- It is a company with more than 100 employees or forms part of a 'group of companies' employing that number of employees.
- The dismissal procedure affects employees with ages above 50 years (at the time their employment contract is terminated) in a proportion higher than the percentage of employees 50 years or older in the workforce. Besides the employees above 50 years of age affected by the collective redundancy procedure, any other employee above 50 or more years whose contract was terminated at the initiative of the company or companies of the same group in response to other motives not inherent to the person of the employee different to those provided for in paragraph (c) of section 1 of section 49 of the Workers' Statute, provided that such terminations of contracts have occurred in the three years prior or one year subsequent to the commencement of the collective dismissal procedure must be included.
- Even when the economic, technical, organizational or production grounds that justify collective dismissals occur, the company or group of companies has posted profits in the two financial years previous to that in which the collective dismissal procedure is commenced, and the company has made a profit in the two years prior to the procedure or becomes profitable for two consecutive years within the four years after the procedure.

The calculation of the economic contribution will take into consideration the amounts of unemployment benefits and subsidies of the employees of 50

24. *Real Decreto 1484/2012*, of 29 October, sets forth the regulation for the contributions to the Public Treasury.

or more years of age affected by the collective dismissal (including social security contributions), but it will also consider any amounts paid to the affected employees as unemployment benefits during procedures of collective suspension of the employment contracts (temporary layoffs or redundancies).

In addition, the rule also states that the said contributions must be made not only on behalf of the employees above 50 years of age affected by the collective redundancy procedure but also on behalf of any other employee (above 50 or more years of age), whose contract was terminated at the initiative of the company or companies of the same group, in response other motives not inherent to the person of the employee different to those provided for in paragraph (c) of section 1 of section 49 of the Workers' Statute, provided that such terminations of contracts have occurred in the three years prior or one year subsequent to the commencement of the collective dismissal procedure.

6.3. Fines and Penalties

Non-compliance with workers' representatives' right to information, consultation, and audience, set forth in the rules of the negotiation period, is a serious infraction, with fines ranging between EUR 751 and EUR 7,500.

Non-compliance with the obligation of presenting the certificate regarding the contribution to the public treasury is a very serious infraction, with fines ranging between EUR 7,501 and EUR 225,018.

6.4. Checklist of Do's and Don'ts

- When downsizing, it is advisable to seek advice from a labour lawyer and an expert on the reasons for downsizing, whether economic or productive, technical or operational.
- Verify all terminations of employees 50 years old carried out in the three years prior to the collective downsizing and carefully plan those in the following year.
- Prepare all the different steps of the procedure well in advance in order to be ready for any situation which may arise.
- Establish a bargaining strategy and avoid deviating from it.
- Contact the senior officers of the trade unions present in the workers' committee in order to facilitate the negotiation. In some occasions, these contacts may be advantageous if established prior to the initiation of the bargaining process.

- It is also advantageous to maintain communication with the administration and the senior officers of the trade union during the bargaining process. Bear in mind that while the legal duration of the negotiation period is thirty days for most companies, in reality, most downsizings last for several months.

7. LABOUR AND EMPLOYMENT LAW RAMIFICATIONS UPON ACQUISITION OR SALE OF A BUSINESS

7.1. Overview

In Spain, the remarkable 'vitality' of the employment contract results in 'conservation of the business' or 'continuity of the contract'. The law (Directive 2001/23/EC, and section 44 of the Workers' Statute) provides the possibility of subjective renovations in the person of the employer, assuming the position of employer a new one, as a party to the existing employment contract. The new employer assumes the obligations of the first one, and the working conditions established by the employment contracts continue. It must be understood that a stock sale does not entail a change in the legal personality of the employer, so it will continue to be the same one. The principle presiding over both our doctrine and our Laws implies that this change of employer due to the transmission of the business or the work centre does not terminate or modify the employment relationship.

7.2. Acquisition of a Business

According to section 44 of the Workers' Statute, a *transfer of undertaking* is deemed to exist when the transfer affects an economic entity that keeps its identity, deemed as a set of measures organized to carry out an economic activity, which is essential or accessory. The transfer may be of an entire company, a work centre or a company's autonomous production unit. That is, not all acquisitions are transfers of undertaking if there is no real transfer of a business.

The employee is transferred with the existing terms and conditions of employment, which include:

- Individual conditions such as position, salary and seniority (years of service since the employment with the transferor started).
- Collective conditions such as those enjoyed as a result of a collective bargaining agreement applicable to the transferor and other collective agreements between the company and its legal representatives. These

conditions also include rights incorporated in the contracts of the employees because of unilateral decisions of the company.
- If there are legal representatives of workers in any of the affected companies, they shall keep their positions.

Therefore, under Spanish legislation, individual rights and obligations arising from an employment contract or from an employment relationship existing on the date of a transfer shall, because of the transfer, be transferred to the transferee. During the transfer process, the transferor or transferee cannot alter the terms of the employment contract. However, after the transfer, the individual or collective employment conditions may be altered, as in any employment relationship, following the legal requirements and limitations.

The transferor and the transferee must provide their respective employee representatives or, if there are no representatives, their respective employees affected by the transfer, the following information (preferably in writing): scheduled date of transfer, reasons for the transfer, legal, economic and corporate consequences of the transfer, and foreseen labour measures, if any (such as downsizings, geographical mobility ...).[25] Failure to provide this information constitutes a serious infraction, punishable with a fine from EUR 751 to EUR 7,500.

However, employees' legal representatives do not have any right to veto or any right to impose conditions on a transfer of undertaking.

The Workers' Statute establishes the obligation to consult the representatives of the employees in good time and prior to the transfer but only if the transferor or the transferee anticipates changes such as a collective transfer, change in the work conditions or collective redundancies. The purpose of the consultation is to reach an agreement. In these cases, the consultancy period must last at least fifteen days.

Both companies (the transferor and the transferee) must file an application form with the Spanish social security authority (the Social Security General Treasury) and submit several compulsory documents, such as the list of affected employees.

Notice must also be given to the Employment Authorities *Servicio Público de Empleo Estatal* (SEPE) by filing a letter stating the assignee undertakes all the transferor's rights and obligations, particularly those related to temporary agreements and special employment agreements.

The new employer shall assume the former employer's rights and obligations for social security matters and any obligations regarding additional social benefits that the transferor may have acquired.

The change of employer is not a cause for termination. If the new employer wants to dismiss a transferred employee merely because of a

25. Section 44 of the Workers' Statute.

change of employer, the termination would be unfair. The new employer would have to pay severance compensation, which would be calculated considering all the years of service for the transferor plus the period of service for the transferee. The procedures for terminations explained in sections 5 and 6 above are applicable in these cases.

The transferor and the transferee are jointly and severally liable for three years from the date of the transfer for all employment liabilities relating to the transferred employees that had arisen before the transfer took place. The general expression 'employment liabilities' includes social security obligations.

The law also provides that the transferor and transferee are jointly and severally liable for the obligations that arise after the transfer if the transfer were declared a crime or fraud.

7.3. Acquisition Checklist

In addition to the mandatory information provision in the Workers' Statute, our regulations impose further duties regarding the information that must be provided to the employee representatives of companies involved in a merger.

These regulations require that the directors of the merging companies draw up a common merger plan (the 'Plan'). They must also prepare a detailed report that justifies the merger, addressing the potential impact on employees, among other considerations.

The Plan, along with the justificatory report and other relevant information, must be made accessible to both the shareholders and the employee representatives—or directly to the employees if there are no representatives—of the companies involved in the merger.

Also, the employee representatives (or the employees themselves, if there are no representatives) have the right to submit their observations on the Plan.

These observations must be presented within five working days before the general shareholders meeting that is convened to approve the merger. They are also given the opportunity to express their views on the report in a timely manner.

7.4. Sale of a Business

See section 7.2 above; these are the same consequences as acquisitions.

7.5. Sale Checklist

See section 7.2 above; these are the same consequences as acquisitions.

8. USE OF ALTERNATIVE WORKFORCES: INDEPENDENT CONTRACTORS, CONTRACT EMPLOYEES, AND TEMPORARY OR LEASED WORKERS

8.1. Overview

In Spain, as in many other countries, alternative workforces are frequently used to reduce costs.

Spanish legislation allows for the use of alternative workforces if several requirements are met.

Most of these requirements seek to provide employment rights to the alternative workforce.

For example, Law 31/1995 for the Prevention of Occupational Hazards establishes obligations for the main employer using alternative workforces, such as ensuring they have received the necessary formation relative to health and safety.

8.2. Independent Contractors

8.2.1. Definition

Independent contractors promote or personally render services or conclude transactions on a regular basis on behalf of the company. They operate independently; their professional services are organized by themselves, and they are not subject to or subordinate to the company's management.[26]

8.2.2. Creating the Relationship

How the parties characterize their relationship in a contract does not determine whether a worker is an employee or an independent contractor. It is important to consider the characteristics of the relationship itself, such as time control and the organization of tasks or schedules. Full dependence on the company would imply an employee relationship, while an employee's

26. *Ley 20/2007*, of 11 July, of Independent Contractors.

autonomous development of activities indicates an independent contractor relationship.

Dependence must be understood as the employer's power to organize in detail the employees' activity and to exercise managerial powers over them. To qualify an employee as an independent contractor, the employer should consider the following practical advice:

(i) Work time: the company should not organize the independent contractor's work time; the contractor is free to organize its daily and weekly schedule.
(ii) Professional organization: an independent agent is an independent businessperson and, as such, is free to develop tasks, holidays, trips, etc., as he or she deems appropriate.
(iii) Reporting obligations: the company may give directions regarding the independent contractor's obligation to report; however, those directions shall not compromise the independence of the contractor's activity, so the obligation to report should not imply full supervision by the company. In practice, reporting obligations must focus on the level of product sales or services rather than typical employment obligations, such as complying with certain working hours.
(iv) Work equipment: ideally, equipment should be provided by the contractor to preserve the contractor's independence.

The platform companies and gig economies and the new ways of work (riders) brought these traditionally defining elements of a labour relationship into the debate and are now being revaluated. After a judgment by the Supreme Court in September 2020, a new law on those relationships was passed in which they are presumed to be employment relationships.

8.2.3. Compensation

Fixed pay and reimbursement of expenses are considered evidence of dependence. However, these types of compensation may exist in a contractor relationship.

The social security regulation establishes that the independent contractor, not the employer, is responsible for the payment of social security contributions.

8.2.4. Other Terms and Conditions

Independent contractors must be registered with the local Value-Added Tax (VAT) and Social Security authorities. However, registration as such is not conclusive of their being independent contractors if the existence of a true employment relationship is proved.

If the company intends to have an independent contractor relationship, the agreement cannot be terminated with dismissal; dismissals are only permitted in labour relationships. Termination clauses in the contract should provide grounds for termination, a notice period, compensation for clients (those with whom the independent contractor should have made deals) and damages, among others.

8.3. CONTRACT WORKERS

The Spanish legal system does not prohibit decentralizing measures and accepts subcontracting of its own activity as licit in section 42 of the Workers' Statute.

The purpose of the contract must be to provide a service, which requires not only providing a labour force, but also organization, equipment, and initiative, with a view to ensuring that the services are provided under both ordinary and extraordinary circumstances.

The contractor (which is frequently a company) negotiates and pays wages and grants time off, leaves and holidays. It imposes disciplinary measures on its employees and applies social security provisions, particularly contributions and payment of benefits. The contractor's staff gives the work orders and instructions on a day-to-day basis.

The contractor exercises its management powers by giving orders as to when, where and how the contracted service will be carried out without the possibility of that management power being appropriated by the company. In the event of lack of compliance, that is, if the company manages and/or pays contract workers, an illegal cession of employees or illegal assignment can be declared, with the consequence explained in section 8.4 below.

Employers have a statutory joint liability for their subcontractor's liabilities. This liability covers the labour and social security rights of the contractor's employees during the time the subcontracting agreement is in force. This obligation continues for one year for labour liabilities after the subcontracting agreement expires and for three years for social security liabilities.[27] Such liability includes payment of employees' salaries and social security contributions, but it does not include compensation for the dismissal of employees.

27. The Social Security joint liability will decay if the Social Security administration does not issue the debts certificate within thirty days of the employer requiring it.

8.4. Leased Workers

Spanish law (section 43 of the Workers' Statute) prohibits the cession or assignment of employees between companies. This is what is called illegal cession of employees.

The consequences of illegally assigning employees are that both the assignor and the assignee will be jointly liable for all obligations to employees and to social security, besides any other liabilities, including criminal (section 312 of the Criminal Code, which forbids workforce trafficking). Workers subject to illegal assignments will be entitled to choose between becoming an employee of the assignor or of the assignee, with entitlement to all the labour privileges established by the applicable collective agreement and all other employment rights offered by the company to its own employees.

Hiring employees to lease them to other companies is only allowed if it is done through TEAs (Temporary Employment Agencies, *Empresas de Trabajo Temporal* (ETT)) duly authorized in the terms established in Law 14/1999, of 1 June, of TEAs.[28]

According to the law, a TEA is a company whose business activity consists of temporarily providing its own employees to another company (the 'user').

The TEA law (section 2.1) establishes that a TEA must comply with the following requirements to obtain compulsory administrative authorization:

- It must have an organized structure that enables it to assume and comply with its obligations.
- Its activity must be exclusively that of TEA.
- It must financially guarantee compliance with salary and social security obligations. This guarantee is a financial guarantee for salary debts resulting from the terminations.
- It has not been penalized by a suspension of its activities in two or more cases.
- It must include in its company name the term 'TEA'.
- TEAs must have a staff of at least twelve employees hired through stable or indefinite-term contracts, both full- and part-time, for every 1,000 employees hired during the previous year. This number of employees (1,000) is the result of the number of days out at the disposal of the user companies divided by 365.

In case of non-compliance with these requirements, the Labour Authority may initiate procedures to partially or totally revoke the administrative authorization of the TEA.

28. The regulation of TEAs is established in Law 14/1999, Directive 200/104/CE and *Real Decreto 4/1995.*

In order to lease employees to the user company, an employee lease contract (*contrato de puesta a disposición*) must be signed between the TEA and the user company. The leased employee will be under the user company's scope of management and administration.

8.4.1. Employee Lease Contract

Employee lease contracts can be executed between TEAs and user companies in the same cases and with the same requirements established for the subscription of temporary employment contracts as described in the employment contract section.

The inexistence of temporary cause justifying temporary employment implies that the lease contract is an illegal cession of employees.

Employee lease contracts cannot be executed:

- for the substitution of employees on strike;
- if the job to be carried out is especially dangerous to health or safety;
- when in the previous twelve months, the company should have eliminated the position for which the employee lease contract was intended through a collective procedure, individual termination for objective reasons, unfair dismissal, or termination at the initiative of the employee (this prohibition does not apply if the objective terminations were due to a major force);
- when in the previous eighteen months, the positions had been covered for more than twelve months, either continuously or discontinuously, by leased employees;
- in order to lease them to other TEAs.

The formal requirements of employee lease contracts are the following:

- Prior to the execution of the contract, the user company will inform the TEA of the characteristics of the position, the roles to be carried out, the risks attached to it and the required abilities of the employee.
- Always in writing and duplicate.
- Its minimum content will include, besides identification of the parties, the cause justifying the execution of the contract, required qualification and content of the job position, risks attached to the position, estimated duration of the employee lease contract, location and working hours, and price agreed between de parties.

User companies must inform the workers' representatives of the subscription of employee lease contracts and the reason for them within ten days of their execution.

8.4.2. Employment Contract Between TEA and Leased Employee

The TEAs hire employees whom they will lease to user companies. The employment contract between the TEA and these employees must be in writing. The duration of the employment contract with the leased employees can be either indefinite or temporary. If it is temporary, the duration must be the same as the employee lease contract executed with the user company.

Nonetheless, it is possible to execute a temporary employment contract with a leasable employee to cover several employee lease contracts with user companies. For this to be valid, the different employee lease contracts must be specified in the employment contract; all of them must cover the temporary needs of the user companies, and the lease contract must comply with all legal requirements.

The temporary employment contracts executed between the TEA and the employee to be leased must include, besides identification of the TEA and the user company, the reason for the employee lease contract, the content of the job, its risks, and the estimated length of the service, location and working hours and the agreed remuneration.

Indefinite-term contracts must have the same content, except that they do not include an estimated length of the service.

8.4.3. Rights and Obligations During the Lease

Leased employees are entitled to the remuneration established in the collective bargaining agreement of the user company for the position covered.

If the contract with the TEA is of a temporary term, the employee will be entitled, upon finalization of the employee lease contract, to severance compensation in the amount of twelve days per year worked.

Leased employees are entitled to the same health and safety protection as the employees of the user company.

Any clause or agreement by which the leased employee must pay an amount to the TEA because of selection, training or hiring is null and void.

TEAs must dedicate 1% of the salary mass of all employees to the training of employees to be leased to user companies.

They must also ensure and provide the leased employees with all necessary formation and training in health and safety, and also all the information regarding the risks associated with the job to be carried out. Compliance with these obligations must be documented.

8.5. Checklist of Do's and Don'ts

- It is illegal to assign a workforce, as opposed to rendering service, except where the company assigning the workforce is registered and authorized to do so. Penalties for illegal assignment of workforce include joint liability for the subcontractors' labour and social security rights (salary and social security contributions), fines and, in exceptional cases, even criminal liability. Subcontractor's employees are entitled to opt to have a labour relationship with the user company or with the contractor. Only registered TEAs are entitled to the assignment of workforce.
- There is an employment relationship when the person rendering the services is subject to the managerial powers of the company, and the company assumes the risks of the business. If a supposed subcontractor complies with these conditions, there will be, in truth, an employment relationship, and the company will be obliged to pay social security and the corresponding salary on equal terms with all other employees.
- Do not disguise employment relationships as subcontracting relationships, as the consequences are the payment of all past social security obligations with a statutory limitation of four years and incorporating the supposed subcontractor into the workforce, plus penalties for the infractions committed (very serious, with a fine of 13.01% to 150% of the amounts not paid).
- Organic Law 14/2022, of 14 December, amended the Criminal Code to punish with prison from six months to six years and fines from six to twelve months, those who impose illegal conditions on their employees by hiring them under formulas that are not part of the employment contract or maintain them against administrative requirement or sanction.

9. OBLIGATIONS TO BARGAIN COLLECTIVELY WITH TRADE UNIONS: EMPLOYEES' RIGHT TO STRIKE AND COMPANY'S RIGHT TO CONTINUE BUSINESS OPERATIONS

9.1. Overview of Unions' Right to Organize

Section 28 of the Spanish Constitution explicitly establishes the right to create trade unions. This freedom includes both the right to found trade unions and the right to join them.

This right is acknowledged in various international treaties to which Spain is a party, such as the Universal Declaration of Human Rights, ILO Standard 87, and the European Convention for the Protection of Human Rights and Fundamental Freedoms.

The right to freely create a trade union also includes the right to establish its organization and ways of operation. The Law of Trade Union Freedom (*Ley Orgánica de Libertad Sindical 11/1986*, of 8 August) grants this right, not to individual workers but collectively to trade union organizations in the exercise of their trade union freedom, that is, their right to unionize.

A consequence of this freedom is that the establishment of the trade union statutes and the acknowledgement of a trade union as a legal entity is not subject to prior permission or administrative authorization.

All workers are entitled to create a trade union, except for military personnel, members of the judiciary and public attorneys. Unemployed workers, autonomous employees (individual independent contractors or self-employed workers) with no employees or retired or disabled employees are entitled to join trade unions, but they are not entitled to create trade unions for the protection and defence of their collective interests. However, they are entitled to create associations (not trade unions) in accordance with specific regulations.

The major Spanish trade union organizations are the General Workers' Union (*Unión General de Trabajadores* (UGT)), which is traditionally linked to the Socialist Party, and the Workers' Commissions (*Comisiones Obreras* (CCOO)), which is linked to the Communist Party. Some trade unions cover certain professions (e.g., SEPLA (*Sindicato Español de Pilotos de Líneas Aéreas*), the trade union of airline pilots) or geographic areas (ELA (*Euskal Langileen Alkartasuna*)); LAB (*Langile Abertzaleen Batzordeak*) trade unions in the Basque Country or CIGA (*Confederación Intersindical Galega*) in Galicia).

It has been common practice in Spain to negotiate tripartite 'social pacts' from time to time. Such political agreements, which are reached by the government, the labour unions and the employers' associations, generally establish the basic framework regarding labour and social policy in the country.

Employers can also be organized, although it is not trade union freedom, which belongs to employees. The largest employers' organization is the Spanish Confederation of Employers' Organizations (*Confederación Española de Organizaciones Empresariales* (CEOE)).

In section 28.2, the Spanish Constitution expressly acknowledges the right of employees to go on strike in defence of their interests. The Strike Law (*Ley de Huelga*) is set forth in *Real Decreto Legislativo 17/1977.*

The judgment of the Constitutional Court 11/1981 established that the essence of the right to strike is the right to stop work (Constitutional Decision 11/1981). This right is not unlimited, and the limits are set, not only in the possible confrontation with other civil rights but also with the possible collision with other interests constitutionally protected. The right of non-striking employees to work is constitutionally protected as another manifestation of union freedom and must be respected. Essential services to the community must also keep functioning. The right to strike does not permit striking employees to occupy the working premises, for example, to stage picket lines or protests, to respect the decision of non-striking employees to keep working.

The decision to go on strike must be adopted by the employees in an assembly or through their representatives, and each employee is entitled to decide individually whether to join the strike. It is not necessary that the strike affects the entire company and workforce.

Employers must be notified of the decision to go on strike at least five calendar days before the date of the initiation of the strike; for companies rendering public services, notification must be given at least ten days in advance. If such a prior notice requirement is not complied with, the strike will be deemed illegal.

The prior notice must contain the following information:

- A statement of the reason and purpose of the strike, sufficiently detailed.
- Different actions are undertaken prior to the strike in order to reach an agreement.
- Date of initiation of the strike. If it is for a limited time, the exact dates of the strike must be specified.
- The composition of the strike committee. The strike committee is in charge of the negotiations during the strike and represents the strikers for the duration of the strike. Its members will be entitled to go to the employer's premises to distribute information about the strike. The strike committee can have a maximum of twelve members.

The employer is entitled to establish, together with the strike committee, safety and maintenance measures during the strike in order to protect the safety of any persons in the company and of its premises, machinery and installations. This will ensure the continuity of the activity once the strike is called off. Employees are obliged to comply with these measures, and such compliance is not considered a violation of their right to strike.

During the strike, the employment relationship with striking employees is suspended, and in consequence, there is neither obligation to work nor to pay salaries during the strike. Employers may not take disciplinary action against employees who join a lawful strike.

Employees who decide not to join the strike must continue rendering their services as usual.

During strikes, the managerial powers of employers are restricted because the exercise of their hiring, organization and disciplinary powers cannot imply a lesion of the employees' right to strike.

Among these restrictions is the prohibition of the employer's replacing striking workers either by external hiring or by making internal substitutions (with employees not on strike). Employers cannot adopt disciplinary measures or make harmful decisions against employees who have gone on strike (e.g., not converting the temporary employment contracts of temporary workers who joined a strike into indefinite-term contracts).

Unlike the right to strike, under Spanish labour law, employers' lockout right is not considered a civil right. While the right to strike is established in section 28.2 of the Constitution, the right to lock out is not expressly covered in the Constitution but is one of the measures considered valid in collective conflicts, in accordance with section 37.2 of the Constitution.

Lockouts can only be used to maintain order or prevent disruption within the company and in any of the following circumstances:

- When there could be a danger to personal life, to physical integrity or to installations or material assets caused by the conflict measures adopted by employees.
- When there is an occupation of the company's premises or immediate danger of its occupation.
- Absences or irregularities in the working process may seriously hinder it.

Lockouts can only last for the time needed to remove their causes and continue the activity and must necessarily affect the entire workforce.

9.2. Right of Employees to Join Unions

Union representatives are elected by employees who are members of the union to represent the union in the company or work centre where the employees are located. The number of union representatives in a company depends on the number of employees it has.

Employees have the statutory right to participate in certain aspects of managing the business in which they are employed, either through the workers' committees or employee delegates. The two types of employee representations are unitary or elective representation; in practice, most employee representatives and works council members are also union representatives.

A company cannot establish a works council; only the workers can. If the workers decide not to call elections, there will be no works council. However, if the employees decide they want a council, the company must provide all the necessary support for setting up a works council.

The powers given to works councils and employees are wide-ranging and include the right to receive information on issues such as the growth of the economic sector to which the company belongs, the company's balance sheets and profit and loss statements; copies of written employment contracts, proposed new employment contracts; statistics on absenteeism and industrial accidents; and any sanctions imposed for serious disciplinary offences.

They are also entitled to issue a report before the company implements decisions involving restructuring the workforce, reviewing or changing organizational systems, or establishing flexitime or shift work. Works councils also monitor the company's compliance with current employment regulations, social security, and labour affairs, and they are responsible for defending employees' interests in relation to risk prevention in the workplace.

Members of a works council and employee representatives have statutorily guaranteed rights, such as the right to priority in a collective redundancy procedure or a formal hearing in case of disciplinary dismissal. In the event of an unfair dismissal, they are also entitled to choose between the termination of their employment with severance compensation and reinstatement in the company.

Company-level agreements are usually negotiated between the works council or the union representatives and the company's management team.

Agreements applying to more than one company must be negotiated by trade unions that:

- are considered 'most representative' at a state-wide level; or
- are considered 'most representative' at an Autonomous Community level in respect of agreements that do not go beyond the geographical area.

The Law of Trade Union Freedom, section 6, establishes that in order to be a 'most representative' trade union, the union must have as members at least 10% of the members of the works council or personnel delegates in the geographic and functional area to which the agreement refers.

Employers' associations, in order to be able to negotiate legitimately, must also count as members at least 10% of the employers within the geographical and functional area to which the agreement refers, as long as those employers have an equal percentage of the affected employees.

9.3. How Employees Select Unions

Employee representatives can be elected in companies or establishments with more than ten, but fewer than fifty employees and where there are between six and ten employees, and a majority decides to have an employee representative.

Works councils may be elected in companies with fifty or more employees.

9.4. Pre-election Campaigning

Pursuant to Spanish labour laws, the election procedure is established in sections 69–77 of the Worker's Statute and in the Regulation for Elections to workers' representatives in Spain (*Reglamento de Elecciones, Real Decreto 1844/1994*, of 9 September) as follows:

- Prior notice of the holding of elections must be issued by the organizers (either unions or the employees) to the company and the public office of the Labour Authority at least one month and not more than three months prior to the commencement of the election procedure. Within seven days of such notice, the company has to give notice of the calling of elections to the workers who are going to form the election committee and, should they exist, to the workers' representatives.
- The election committee is formed on the date established by the organizers in their prior notice.
- The election committee creates a census of electors. Spanish law does not establish a deadline for the census. However, the census is usually drawn up by the committee within twenty-four to forty-eight hours after the formation of the election committee.
- The list of electors is published and displayed on the company notice board for a period of not less than seventy-two hours.
- Up to twenty-four hours after the period during which the list of electors is displayed, the committee has to resolve any problem or claim raised in relation to inclusions, exclusions or corrections.
- The definitive list of electors is published within twenty-four hours from the end of the period for resolution of claims: the number of members of the works council to be elected is then established.
- Candidates are presented within nine days from the definitive publication of the list of electors in the form provided in the Regulation for Elections. The committee announces the candidatures by publishing a list of candidates on the notice board within two working days from the conclusion of the period for presenting candidates. The committee's announcement may be challenged within the next working day, and the committee must decide on the challenges on the next working day.
- The election campaign is conducted from the definitive announcement of the candidates until midnight prior to the ballot. At least five days must elapse between the announcement of candidates and the ballot.
- Immediately following the ballot, which is held on the date established by the election committee, the results are assigned by the election committee. The election committee has three working days to draw up a record of the votes. The results are published within twenty-four hours from the drawing up of the overall record of the count.

- The record of the ballot must be then presented within three working days to the competent public office of the Labour Authority. This office, on a working day immediately following such presentation, must complete the record and publish it on the notice board.
- When ten working days have elapsed from the publication on the notice board, the public office of the Labour Authority will register the election records. Not registering the results is only allowed when the following requirements have not been complied with: the records are not on the official forms, lack of notification of the election process to the Labour Authority, absence of signature of the election committee's president, and omission or ineligibility of data that should render impossible the ballot.

9.5. Unfair Labour Practices

Punishing or dismissing an employee representative due to the employee's representative activity is not allowed, and disciplinary measures and/or termination will be declared null and void.

Non-compliance with workers' representatives' rights to information, consultation and audience is a serious infraction and fined an amount ranging between EUR 751 and EUR 7,500.

9.6. Relocation of Work/Shutdown of Business

Employee representatives are entitled to issue a report before the company implements decisions involving a restructuring of the workforce by means of a partial restructuring or the shutdown of business.

9.7. Checklist of Do's and Don'ts

The members of the works council are protected from unfair persecution by the company based on their union activities by certain guarantees so that they can carry out their duties. The guarantees are as follows:

- If the company wants to penalize an employee representative for a serious or very serious breach of contract, a formal procedure must be followed during which the employee may file an opposition. The company has to inform the works council of its intention to penalize the employee, explaining all facts in detail so the works council can defend the accused representative. Once this procedure is finished, the company shall decide whether to apply the disciplinary measure. If the company penalizes the employee without going through this procedure, the disciplinary measure shall be deemed contrary to law.

- Typically, if an employee is unfairly dismissed, the company decides whether to reinstate the employee or pay severance pay. An employee representative who is unfairly dismissed may choose between these alternatives.
- When employment is terminated for economic, productive, or other objective causes, employee representatives have priority over other employees to keep their jobs.
- The workers' council has the right to freely express its opinions on matters related to the scope of its representation. It can publish and distribute any material of interest as long this activity does not interfere with the company's operation. It is not required to notify or pre-notify the company of any of these actions.
- Each member of the works council is entitled to a number of paid hours off per month to carry out representative duties.
- The company must provide an adequate place/room for the works council to carry out its activities and to meet with the staff, as well as a notice board in the work centre for its publications.

10. WORKING CONDITIONS: HOURS OF WORK AND PAYMENT OF WAGES – BY STATUTE OR COLLECTIVE AGREEMENTS

10.1. Overview of Wage and Hours Laws

The length of the workday is established in collective agreements or individual employment contracts.

Section 34 of the Workers' Statute sets the maximum working hours at forty hours a week, based on a twelve-month period, although collective agreements may vary on these terms.

Collective agreements or individual company agreements may provide for working hours to vary in their distribution throughout the year if the minimum daily and weekly rest periods envisaged by laws[29] are respected. Unless otherwise set forth by collective agreements, the company may distribute irregularly up to 10% of the yearly working time.

There must be a minimum of twelve hours between the end of one working day and the start of the next. The number of hours worked per day may not exceed nine unless the collective agreement or individual company

29. The Workers' Statute, ss 12.5 and 34.7 and Special Working Hours Decree (*Real Decreto 1561/1995*, of 21 September, *sobre jornadas especiales de trabajo*).

agreement establishes a different working pattern for the day. In all cases, however, the rest between working days must be respected.

Companies are obliged to keep a register of each employee's standard working day with their start and finish times and keep the said register for four years.

10.2. Minimum Wage

The Spanish Constitution (section 35) provides that all Spaniards are entitled to sufficient wages to meet their needs and their families' needs. To ensure that this principle is applied, a basic minimum wage has been introduced and is established every year following consultation with representative unions and employers' associations. The fixed minimum rates consider, amongst other things, the retail price index, average national productivity, and the general economic climate. The rates are reviewed every six months against the retail price index forecasts.

The minimum wage for 2024 is fixed at EUR 1,134 per month in fourteen monthly instalments (EUR 15,876 per year). In practice, salaries usually exceed the minimum established by the government, either due to collective bargaining (wage rates are one of the key issues negotiated by trade unions) or through direct negotiation between the employer and the employee.

Salaries should not be below the minimum salary provided for the particular job category in the collective bargaining agreement. There is also the national minimum daily and monthly wage, which is set each year. Employees are entitled to two mandatory monthly extraordinary payments each year, one in December and the other in July. This means that to calculate an employee's monthly payments, the yearly remuneration must be divided by fourteen instead of twelve. It is important to remember this when making the relevant monthly instalments.

Some collective agreements allow for only twelve payments, so the total that would be paid in fourteen payments is only paid in twelve. If this is the case, and the employee only receives twelve monthly payments, each monthly payment (the twelve of them) sheet should specifically show the amount corresponding to the two extra monthly payments. Remuneration in kind may not exceed 30% of the employee's salary.

10.3. Overtime

Hours worked in excess of the forty hours established in section 34 of the Workers' Statute or the maximum number of working hours set forth in collective bargaining agreements are considered overtime. No more than eighty overtime hours may be worked annually. Overtime may be compensated with time off or paid at a rate of at least the same amount paid for regular hours. Collective agreements or individual contracts establish whether overtime will be paid at an increased rate or compensated with paid time off. Overtime is voluntary.

10.4. Right to Disconnect

Employees are entitled to disconnect from digital devices during off-work hours to ensure respect for their rest time, holidays and privacy.

The law calls on employers, after hearing from workers' representatives, to set up internal policies defining for employees how to exercise the right to disconnect, including training for staff on reasonable use of technology to help avoid computer fatigue. Spain's law emphasizes that employees working remotely are guaranteed the right to disconnect.

10.5. Meal and Rest Periods

There must be a minimum of twelve hours between the end of one working day and the start of the next. The number of hours of effective work per day may not exceed nine hours.

When the length of continuous working days exceeds six hours, a rest period of at least fifteen minutes must be granted.

Workers are entitled to a minimum weekly rest period of uninterrupted one-and-a-half days, which may be accumulated for periods of up to fourteen days. This rest period is usually taken on Saturday evenings (or, in some cases, Monday mornings) and all day Sunday.

10.6. Deductions from Wages

Both the company and the employees must make monthly payments (contributions) to the Social Security Treasury. These contributions are also called quotas.

The employer is responsible for the submission of both contributions (the company's part and the employee's part). The employee's contribution is withheld from the monthly salary as a deduction. The payment must be made before the end of the month following the month they correspond to; in other words, the payment for June must be made by 31 July.

Withholdings for social security are used to cover public payments for illnesses, work-related accidents and work-related illnesses, salary guarantee funds, unemployment, professional education, and overtime.

The monthly payment, or quota, is a percentage of the total salary the employee earns from the company. The base of contribution to which the percentage is applied is capped for 2024 at a maximum of EUR 4,720.50 per month. This means any amounts earned over that cap will not be subject to social security contributions.

Table 1 shows the percentages for 2024:

Table 1 Percentage of Social Security Deductions for 2024

Contingency	*Employer (%)*	*Employee (%)*	*Total (%)*
Common Contingencies*	23.6	4.7	28.3
Unemployment	5.50	1.55	7.05
Salary Guarantee Fund	0.2	–	0.2
Professional Education	0.6	0.1	0.7
Intergenerational Equity Mechanism	*0.58*	*0.12*	*0.7*
Total	*29.9*	*6.35*	*36.25*

* Common contingencies are retirement, disability, widow's pension, death, etc. unemployment, salary guarantee fund and professional training.

Besides the above contingencies and percentages, there is also a contribution for professional contingencies, which varies substantially depending on the degree of risk of the activity performed by the company or the specific risks of the employee's job. There is a list of professions with their corresponding risk tariffs that are used to quantify the contribution to Social Security.

Temporary contracts lasting less than thirty days are subject to an additional social security contribution of EUR 26.6.

Regarding the withholding tax, it is an individual contribution of the employee, but the employer is obliged to withhold a specific percentage from the employee's monthly salary and submit it to the tax authorities. The percentage varies according to the employee's annual salary and family circumstances. The applicable rate is applied to the employee's full salary, including remuneration in kind.

10.7. Garnishment

The Workers' Statute (section 27.2) establishes that garnishment of employees' salaries cannot reduce the salary to below the minimum wage fixed each year. The amounts exceeding the minimum wage could be subject to garnishment following a percentage scale and taking into account the employee's familial circumstances, as set forth in the *Ley de Enjuciamiento Civil* (General Civil Procedural Law).

10.8. Exemptions to Wage and Hour Laws

The parties may agree to better hour and wage conditions than the ones established in the bargaining agreements and the Workers' Statute.

Usually, qualified employees (managers, top managers, etc.) agree to receive an annual bonus based on performance, that is, on their management efficiency or on the company's results.

Managers are not usually subject to set working hours due to the obligation to perform their duties efficiently and with dedication, as long as the company's rules for personnel rest time are considered.

10.9. Child Labour

The statutory minimum age for employing children is sixteen years. The law also prohibits the employment of persons under the age of eighteen at night, for overtime work, or in sectors considered hazardous (mining, explosives industries, etc.).

10.10. Recordkeeping Requirements

10.10.1. Information That Must Be Maintained

- *Payroll information*: Name and any identifying number or symbol, such as the National Identity Number or Foreigner Identification Number and the Number of Affiliation to the Social Security; home address; date of birth; gender; occupation; employment dates; time and day workweek begins and ends; regular pay rate; hours worked each work day and each workweek; total daily or weekly straight-time earnings; total overtime earnings, total wages paid each pay period; date of payment; pay period covered, the location where work is performed; cause for discharge or

voluntary termination; additions to or deductions from wages in each pay period, including dates, amounts, and the type of additions or deductions.
- Even though for employment-related purposes, the limitation period for keeping such records is only one year, due to the impact on potential income tax withholdings or social security contributions, such information should be stored for the limitation period for tax and social security (four fiscal years).
- Register of the standard working day for each employee with the start and finish times.
- Register of the disaggregated salary information by gender and professional classification. This register is accessible to employees' legal representatives and to employees through their legal representatives, and all employees carrying out equal-value jobs must receive the same salary.
- *Personnel records*: Job applications, resumes, records related to failure/refusal to hire, promotions, demotions, transfers, layoffs, recall, discharge, rates of pay and selection for training. If the candidates are actually hired – either for an indefinite term or for a temporary period – the company must store personnel records while the employment is in force and for the limitation period after the termination of employment (at least one year after termination and, ideally, two to three years after termination). If the candidate is not hired, the company must delete and cancel the personnel records as soon as practicable after the decision not to hire the candidate has been made.
- *Physical examinations*: Health and safety provisions require the employer to accommodate the job position to the health of the employee and abilities of the employee. This information is required to be stored while the employment is in force and for the limitation period after the termination of employment (at least one year after termination, ideally two to three years after termination).

10.10.2. Records That Must Be Retained

- Social security records for at least four years.
- Pay stubs.
- Employment contracts.
- Tax withholdings.
- Daily working hours.
- Health and safety evaluations, controls, check-ups, investigations or reports on health and safety issues, namely safety hazards planning, risk evaluation and planning of preventive activities, and health monitoring (physical evaluations).

- Registry book of contractors rendering services for the company on the company's premises.
- Registration of visits from the Labour and Social Security Inspectors.
- Registry of all information received through the whistleblowing system.

10.10.3. Failure to Maintain Required Records

The consequences of failing to maintain required records are established in the *Real Decreto Legislativo 5/2000*, of 4 August, of infractions and penalties in labour relations.

Failure to maintain social security records for four years constitutes a minor infraction, punishable by a fine ranging between EUR 70 and EUR 750.

Failure to record and file the data obtained in the evaluations, controls, check-ups, investigations or reports on health and safety issues, namely safety hazards planning, risk evaluation and planning of preventive activities, and health monitoring (physical evaluations), is a serious infraction of the employer's obligations and may be fined from EUR 2,451 to EUR 49,180.

Failure to have the required book of visits of the Labour and Social Security Inspections in the work centre is a minor infraction, punishable by a fine of EUR 70 to EUR 750. Non-compliance with formal or documental obligations is also a minor infraction.

Failure to register daily working time constitutes a serious infraction, punishable by a fine ranging between EUR 751 and EUR 7,500.

Failure to register information received through the whistleblowing system constitutes a minor infraction, punishable by fines to legal entities of up to EUR 100,000 and to individual people with fines from EUR 1,001 to EUR 10,000.

10.11. Reductions in Compensation Caused by Economic Downturn

The substance of a contract, once made, cannot be modified unilaterally without cause by one of the contracting parties, either by an express statement or by the subsequent behaviour of either party.

The employer may reduce salaries with the written consent of each employee involved in the wage reduction or when objective reasons concur.

In consequence, if there is a cause, employers can modify terms of employment, including compensation.

Sections 41 and 82 of the Workers' Statute enable employers to modify terms of employment. The scope of application of each section depends on whether the terms of employment to be modified are established in the employment contract or company agreements or in collective bargaining agreements published in the Official Bulletins (*see* section 1).

Both procedures must be based on objective causes; economic, technical, productive, or organizational, and the employer must provide evidence of the reasons justifying the modification. These causes are like the ones justifying redundancies but more flexible.

Under the *substantial modification of labour conditions* provisions in section 41 of the Workers' Statute, the employer may modify the terms of the employment (including compensation) for economic, technical, organizational or productive reasons as long as these terms of employment are not set forth in collective bargaining agreements and are related to competitiveness, productivity, or technical or work organization of the company. Failure to follow this procedure constitutes a serious infraction, punishable with a fine from EUR 751 to EUR 7,500.

The procedure is different depending on the substantial modification being individual or collective.

The modification is collective if, within a ninety-day period, it affects:

- At least ten employees in a company of less than 100 employees.
- At least 10% of the employees in companies with between 100 and 300 hundred employees.
- At least thirty employees in companies with 300 or more employees.

If the number of employees affected is below these thresholds, the procedure will have to be carried out following the procedure for individual modifications. This procedure requires written notification to the employee with prior notice of fifteen days.

Employees affected by the modification may accept it, challenge it, or terminate the employment contract with a severance compensation of twenty days' salary per year worked up to a maximum of nine monthly instalments.

When the substantial modification is collective, a negotiation period with the workers' representatives is required for a maximum of fifteen days, depending on the number of employees in the workforce and if there are employee representatives in all the work centres. If the parties do not reach an agreement, the employer may unilaterally impose the modification, giving a prior notice of seven days before the modification becomes effective.

The substantial modifications of labour conditions as provisioned in section 41 of the Workers' Statute may be of an indefinite term.

If the terms of employment – including salary amounts – to be modified are set forth in a collective bargaining agreement, the procedure *for the non-application of collective bargaining agreements* to be followed is set forth in section 82.3 of the Workers' Statute. This procedure requires a negotiation period with the workers' representatives. The duration of the modification is limited to the term of the modified collective bargaining agreement. If there is no agreement, the Law sets forth a complex system of mediation to promote a solution between the parties. If no agreement is reached, the employer is not entitled to impose the change unilaterally.

The causes on which the non-application of a collective bargaining agreement must be based are economic, technical, organizational or productive.

Regarding economic grounds, under law, there must be a negative economic situation, current or foreseen; 'a persistent decrease in income or sales' is evidence of such a situation. The reform considers a decrease in income or sales to be persistent if it takes place during two consecutive quarters compared to the same quarters of the previous year.

As for productive, technical, and organizational grounds, the law no longer requires companies to prove the reasonability of the dismissal as a measure to prevent companies' negative performances. These reasons are defined as follows:

- Technical: changes, among others, on the production means or tools.
- Organizational: changes, among others, in the work systems or methods or in the production organization.
- Productive: changes, among others, in demand for products or services that the company wants to sell in the market.

10.12. Temporary Redundancy Plans: Suspension of Employment Contracts or Reductions in Working Time

Besides these two alternatives of reduction of employment costs, section 47 of the Workers' Statute permits reduction through the temporary suspension of employment contracts or temporary reduction of working time (between 10% and 70%) based either on force majeure grounds or on economic, technical and organizational grounds.

These procedures are applicable regardless of the number of employees affected.

If based on force majeure grounds, no negotiation period is required, and it must be requested from the Labour Authority, which must give an answer within five days.

If based on business-related grounds, a negotiated procedure must be followed, very similar to the one set forth in the case of section 41 of the Workers' Statute, seen above.

During the suspension/reduction of employees on whichever grounds, affected employees are entitled to unemployment benefits.

There is no obligation to work nor to pay salaries, but companies are obliged to make social security contributions during the length of the temporary redundancy plan.

These procedures were very much applied during the COVID-19 crisis in 2020 and 2021, and certain measures were adopted to ease the consequences on both affected employees and companies, on unemployment benefits and exemptions on contribution to social security and through a shortening of the length of the procedures if due to COVID-19. Employers enjoying exemptions on social security contributions must maintain employment for six months after the end of temporary redundancy plans.

10.13. Checklist of Do's and Don'ts

- To avoid litigation, it is advisable to only modify an employment agreement with the consent of employees.
- In order to more easily modify working conditions when necessary, draft employment contracts that envisage that possibility as much as legally possible in relation to working time, functions and the working system. In some cases, it might be convenient to explore the possibility of establishing in the employment contract the circumstances that would enable the company to modify the employment contract.
- Negotiation and obtaining consent may be facilitated by the imposition of a time limit for the modification.
- It is advisable to keep records longer than the statutory period in order to better prove the company's labour employment practices in the event of an inspection; however, the obligations set forth in the Data Protection Law must be taken into account.

11. OTHER WORKING CONDITIONS AND BENEFITS: BY STATUTE, COLLECTIVE AGREEMENTS OR COMPANY POLICY

11.1. Health and Other Insurance

Employees are not entitled to health or other types of insurance besides the mandatory public social security system or benefits granted through employment contracts or collective bargaining agreements.

The Spanish social security system offers a wide range of benefits, including medical care, benefits for dependent children, death benefits to survivors, unemployment allowances, retirement pensions, temporary or permanent disability grants, and maternity benefits.

However, it is not unusual for companies to pay voluntarily for additional benefits such as life insurance or private medical insurance.

11.2. Pension and Retirement Benefits

The public Social Security system provides retirement pensions to employees who:

- have reached 67 years of age;
- have been making contributions for a minimum of fifteen years, of which at least two must be within the fifteen years immediately before the date the right accrued, that is, when the age required for retirement is reached.

The minimum retirement age is the same for men and women. The government may lower the retirement age for professional groups or activities where the work is exceptionally physically demanding, toxic, dangerous or unhealthy and has high mortality rates, such as miners, firefighters, train drivers, pilots, artists, maritime employees, etc.).

Retirement pensions (in contributory form) are based on the contributions made by the individual during the 300 months immediately previous to the date the pension is payable, divided by 350. The contributions for the twenty-four months preceding the date on which the pension becomes payable are calculated on their nominal value, while all others are revised in line with the retail price index.

People aged 65 and over who do not have sufficient resources and who are legally resident in Spanish territory could be entitled to a non-contributory retirement pension when they do not comply with all the requirements to obtain a contributory pension under the above-mentioned terms.

Apart from the national social security system, Spanish pension laws (*Real Decreto Legislativo 1/2002*, of 29 November, establishing the regulation of Pension Plans and Funds and Social Security Law) also provide the regulation for private pension systems, designed to be implemented in companies or group of companies, to enhance the personal savings in the framework of employment relationships.

11.3. Vacation and Holiday Payments on Termination

In addition to public holidays, employees are entitled to annual paid leave of at least thirty calendar days per year (section 38 of the Workers' Statute).

Vacation should be taken during the work year. It is generally not possible to accumulate vacation from year to year or to receive payment for unused vacation time, except in the event of termination.

When vacation time is to be taken must be agreed upon between the employee and employer, and there is a special judicial procedure to quickly resolve any potential conflicts over the dates of enjoyment.

In Spain, there are fourteen public holidays per year, including two days for local holidays. The key public holidays are Christmas Day, New Year's Day, Labour Day (1 May), and Spain's National Day (12 October).

11.4. Leaves of Absence

11.4.1. Personal Leave

Section 37 of the Workers' Statute sets out employees' right to paid leave in certain situations, provided they give advance notice to the employer and the time off is legitimate. Allowable paid leaves include:

- Fifteen calendar days when the employee gets married or registers a domestic partnership.
- Five days for serious accidents or diseases, hospitalization or surgery without hospitalization requiring home rest for the spouse, the common-law partner, or any family member up to the second degree of consanguinity or affinity, including those of the common-law partner and cohabiting persons who require the effective care of the worker.
- One day for moving residence.
- Time needed for unavoidable personal or public duty (including voting in elections).
- Time needed to carry out union duties or staff representation under the terms established by law or collective agreement.
- Time needed for antenatal examinations and antenatal/parentcraft classes.
- For force majeure situations due to unforeseeable urgent reasons related to family members or cohabitating persons in the event of a disease or accident that requires immediate presence. This paid leave is given for a number of hours equivalent to four days per year, as provided under the applicable collective agreement, and the worker must provide proof of the reason for the absence.
- A new ground has been approved for the suspension of the labour relationship (called parental leave) for up to eight weeks, which can be enjoyed continuously or with interruption until the child or foster child reaches eight years of age. At the moment, this leave is unpaid.

The amount of leave may be increased by collective bargaining or individual employment agreements.

11.4.2. Medical or Sick Leave

Employees are entitled to sick leave when a doctor from the Social Security public health service diagnoses the sickness and considers that it disables the employee from work. During sick leave, employees are entitled to a public subsidy covering part of their salary. Some collective bargaining agreements establish additional sick pay of up to 100% of the regular salary, payable by the employer.

Sick pay covers the employee from the fourth day of leave onwards. The employer is responsible for sick pay from the fourth day through the fifteenth day, and Social Security is responsible from the sixteenth day onwards. From the first day to the fourth, the employee is not entitled to any payment from the employer or from Social Security.

As of 1 June 2023, this does not apply in case of sick leave due to secondary incapacitating menstruation;[30] due to interruption of pregnancy, whether voluntary or not, unless it is the result of an accident at work or occupational disease; or due to gestation of the working woman from the first day of the thirty-ninth week. In these cases, the affected women are entitled to sick pay from Social Security from the outset.

The amount of the public subsidy is 60% of the base contribution to social security between the fourth and the twentieth day of the sick leave, and from the twenty-first day onwards, it is 75% of the contribution base to Social Security.

To be entitled to sick pay, an employee must have contributed to social security for at least one hundred eighty days within the previous five years, unless the leave is required due to an accident at work or an illness related to the employee's profession, in which no prior contribution period is required. As of 1 June 2023, this requirement does not apply in case of sick leave due to the above-mentioned secondary incapacitating menstruation or due to interruption of pregnancy, whether voluntary or not.

The maximum duration of benefits for a temporary disability due to illness or accident is twelve months. An additional six months of benefits may be granted if it is anticipated that the worker may recover during that period.

If the employee does not recover within the maximum period of eighteen months on temporary disability, the employee will be medically examined to determine the level of disability and may be declared permanently disabled at the following levels:

30. According to the Law, it is 'the situation of incapacity derived from dysmenorrhea generated by a previously diagnosed pathology'.

- partial disability for the employee's profession or job;
- total disability for the employee's profession;
- absolute disability for any kind of work and grand invalidity.

All of them imply the termination of the employment relationship except for the partial disability for the employee's position or job, which requires at least 33% disability of the employee and the ability to perform the fundamental duties of the job position. In case of disability for the employee's profession or job, as a result of a decision by the European Court of Justice, the Workers' Statute will be amended so employers will be required to make reasonable adjustments in order to facilitate the employee a position, unless it is too onerous or inviable, prior to terminating the employment relationship.

In special cases, the determination of the employee's disability can be delayed for up to thirty months from the beginning of the temporary disability.

Once the employee has recovered, the employee has the right to be reinstated in the same position the employee held before the sick leave.

11.4.3. Bereavement Leave

Employees are entitled to two days' leave for the death of relatives up to twice removed, which could be extended to four days if the employee needs to travel to a different province from their place of residence. Some collective bargaining agreements establish longer periods for closer relatives.

11.4.4. Family Leave

The Workers' Statute establishes that employees are also entitled to reduce working hours (by 12.5%–50%) with a proportional reduction in salary to take care of children less than 12 years of age or disabled relatives.

Also, the same law establishes that parents or legal guardians may take up to three years' unpaid leave for the care of children counted from the date of birth or adoption of the child, with their individual job position reserved for the first year and with a reserve of a similar job position for the second and third years.

11.4.5. Pregnancy Leave

Among the paid leaves, it is established that during pregnancy, employees may attend the necessary medical examinations (antenatal exams, birth preparation, etc.).

In addition, social security regulation provides specific pregnancy leaves for situations in which the job may pose risks for the pregnant employee or for the baby. Health and safety provisions[31] require the employer to offer a new position to the pregnant employee in these situations, so this pregnancy leave will only apply when the company has no suitable positions for the pregnant employee.

Pregnant employees on leave because of health risks either to the child or the mother are entitled to a public subsidy equal to 100% of their base contribution to Social Security.

11.4.6. Suspension Due to Childbirth

The term of the suspension of the employment agreement due to childbirth for the biological mother is sixteen weeks long. The six weeks immediately after childbirth will be mandatory and must be uninterrupted and full-time.

The suspension for the parent other than the biological mother is also sixteen weeks, of which the six weeks immediately after childbirth will be mandatory and must be uninterrupted and full-time.

After the first six weeks immediately after childbirth, the ten remaining weeks can be distributed as the parents wish in weekly periods, to be taken cumulatively or intermittently, full-time or part-time, from the end of the mandatory suspension after childbirth until the child is twelve months old. Each weekly period, or, as the case may be, the accumulation of those periods, must be notified to the company at least fifteen days in advance.

This suspension may be in full-time or part-time terms once an agreement between the company and the employee is reached.

Likewise, suspension due to adoption, custody for adoption, and fostering has a sixteen-week term per adopting or fostering parent, six of which are mandatory and must be taken full-time and uninterruptedly following the court or administrative ruling.

The term of the suspension is increased where there are:

- multiple births (by two weeks for each additional child, to be counted from the second child); or

31. *Real Decreto 295/2009*, of 6 March, of Social Security provisions for maternity, paternity, risk during pregnancy and lactation and *Ley 31/1995,* of 8 November, for the Prevention of Occupational Hazards.

– medical complications.

Pregnant employees and those who have recently given birth are entitled to time off for, among other things, attending antenatal clinics and breastfeeding, in addition to the sixteen weeks' suspension leave.

Social security benefits are paid to employees whose contracts of employment have been suspended because of childbirth.

The monthly benefit is equal to 100% of the base contribution to social security.

11.4.7. Injury at Work

Injuries caused by working conditions are treated as industrial accidents; it is necessary to analyse the cause to determine the company's responsibility and to adapt the labour prevention plans in order to avoid future accidents.

When a work accident or profession-related illness results in sick leave, the public payment for sick leave comes into effect on the first day of leave, and the amount is 75% of the base of contribution to the Social Security. The duration limits are the same as for ordinary sick leaves.

11.5. Checklist of Do's and Don'ts

- Comply with all the regulations on benefits and leaves established by agreements. Granting excess benefits may be considered a concession by the company to improve employees' rights and cannot be eliminated unilaterally without cause.
- Establish a simple and straightforward procedure for soliciting paid leaves and requesting leaves of absence, as it will facilitate their control and management by the company.
- Require employees to provide documentation of the reason for the permits and leaves of absence, for example, a contract with the moving company or a birth certificate.
- In cases of sickness, be strict about monitoring the employee's situation without invading the employee's or the family's sensitivities and privacy.

12. WORKERS' COMPENSATION

12.1. Overview

Apart from an annual fixed salary, employees may be entitled to additional amounts under a wide variety of salary schemes.

Incentives can be based on individual and/or company performance, subject to the rules of the agreed scheme. The scheme rules must state whether the incentive is to become a permanent benefit under the contract or whether it is temporary, such as for one year. Employers also need to state whether such schemes are discretionary, that is, incentives can be granted to some employees – as long as the distinction is not based on discriminatory grounds – but not others, and that they may vary or even may be terminated or established only for a certain period of time or for a certain occasion.

Salary incentives may be established in individual employment contracts or in a collective bargaining agreement.

Salary may be paid in cash or in kind, such as a car or accommodation; however, the proportion of salary to be paid in kind cannot exceed 30% of the employee's total wages.

Certain employees, especially those at the management level, receive additional benefits, such as company cars, mobile telephones, and private health insurance. Generally, payments in kind are subject to income tax based on their normal market value. There are, however, specific rules for valuing the most common types of payment in kind. For example, the tax to be withheld on the use of a car depends on whether the car is the property of the company or leased.

12.2. Checklist of Do's and Don'ts

- It is advisable to have a clear and simple compensation policy to avoid possible misunderstandings and expectations.
- The same salary must be paid to employees carrying out equal-value jobs under the parameters defined by the law.
- Avoid granting variable compensation plans that commit the company to more than one year since circumstances may vary, as it is more convenient to establish them yearly.
- Be very strict about complying with all tax requirements.
- Adequately compensate competent employees in order to retain them. In some sectors, granting participation in the business gives a sense of entitlement and increases employee motivation and dedication.
- Beware of the impact that additional compensation may have on severance payment requirements. For example, stock options are considered salary, and granting such options may, in some cases, greatly increase the severance compensation costs.

13. COMPANY'S OBLIGATION TO PROVIDE SAFE AND HEALTHY WORKPLACE

13.1. Overview of Safety and Environmental Laws and Regulations

The basic regulation on health and safety in the workplace in Spain is the Law for the Prevention of Occupational Hazards 31/1995, dated 8 November 1995 (*Ley de Prevención de Riesgos Laborales*), which provides a full range of obligations and responsibilities for employers and employees. There are no environmental laws relating to working conditions in Spain.

According to the Prevention of Occupational Hazards Law, within an organization, responsibility for risk prevention may be undertaken by:

- the employer;
- specific employees;
- a risk-prevention department;
- a joint risk-prevention service set up with other employers; or
- an external risk-prevention service.

The employer must set up a risk-prevention department in any of the following situations:

- a company has more than five hundred employees;
- companies which have between two hundred and fifty and five hundred employees that carry out hazardous activities;
- when the employment authorities have decided the employer is obliged to have such a department because of the dangerous activity of the company or the frequency of work accidents, subject to a report by the Labour Inspector and, if relevant, the technical experts involved in risk-prevention issues unless the company has already entered into a contract with an external risk-prevention service.

In cases where an employer is not obliged to establish a risk-prevention department but lacks sufficient resources to provide a proper risk-prevention service, the employer must appoint an external organization to provide risk-prevention services.

Companies or workplaces with fifty or more employees must have a health and safety committee. The health and safety committee is a 'parity' committee whose members consist equally of employee and employer representatives. Its function is to be periodically consulted on the issue of risk prevention in the company. Union representatives and technical risk-prevention managers in the company may participate verbally, but they cannot vote in committee meetings.

Finally, employers are obliged to consult with employee representatives regarding decisions that may have an impact on health and safety in the workforce.

13.2. Requirements

Health and Safety regulations are numerous and complex. These general regulations are subject to continuous modifications to cover new risks detected and to make working conditions more adequate to protect employees. The most recent rules have focused on organizing health and safety schemes for contractors and subcontractors, specifically in the building sector.

13.3. Rights of Employees

All employees are legally entitled to health and safety at work and to be protected by the public health and safety authorities (such as bodies of prevention technicians specifically created in some Autonomous Communities). Also, employers have a duty to protect employees from occupational risks. The employer must take care of its employees with the 'care of a good *pater familias*'.

According to the Occupational Hazards Law, employers must guarantee the health and safety of their employees in all aspects of their work by taking necessary preventative action and by adopting and regularly updating appropriate health and safety measures. These should be aimed at avoiding risks, that is, evaluating those that are inevitable and taking measures to reduce or eliminate them; adapting the work to the employee (particularly with respect to monotonous and repetitive work); keeping up with technological advancement; planning prevention; putting collective protection before individual protection; and providing workers with appropriate supervision.

Where employees from two separate organizations work together, both employers have an obligation to communicate and cooperate to identify risks and ensure the implementation of preventative measures.

Furthermore, employers have a responsibility to consider employees' professional skills and experience in matters of health and safety before entrusting them with certain tasks. They must assign jobs that involve specific risks or hazards only to those who have the necessary knowledge or expertise.

Employers must carry out periodical risk assessments, not only to identify the risks and hazards to which their employees are exposed but also to enable them to devise a policy on how to minimize or eliminate those risks.

Employers must inform their employees of any risks (risks that are both general to the company and specific to the jobs), the protection and prevention measures that are applicable to them, and any other emergency measures in place in the company. In addition, employers must provide each employee with theoretical and practical training on health and safety issues relevant to the risks of their particular job.

Sexual violence shall be included among the concurrent occupational risks in the risk assessment of the different jobs occupied by female workers, and companies shall train and inform their female workers accordingly.

Employers also must plan for possible emergencies and adopt measures relating to first aid, firefighting and evacuation. They must appoint specific staff to these tasks, provide them with the necessary training, and periodically check that the adopted measures are working correctly.

Measures must be adopted to stop activities that pose serious health or safety risks. Employers also must periodically check on their employees' health in relation to risks inherent in the work, subject to the employee's consent.

Employers have a statutory duty to develop and make available to the appropriate labour authorities documents demonstrating compliance with their health and safety obligations.

13.4. Rights of Employer

The Law for the Prevention of Occupational Hazards also establishes obligations for employees, who must follow all the preventive procedures established in the workplace. They must use safety clothing and equipment appropriately and receive specific training on health, safety, and emergency procedures.

Employers are entitled to adopt disciplinary measures to force employees to follow procedures, and the failure to enforce employees' compliance with the safety measures could be considered a failure of the employer's obligations to safety.

Workers must protect their own health and safety as much as possible and the health and safety of other workers. Specifically, employees must:

- use machines, tools, dangerous substances, equipment and other working material properly;
- use safety devices adequately in the workplace;

- immediately inform the employer (or the workers appointed in the company to carry out protection and prevention activities, as well as the prevention service) about any situation that could involve a possible risk to the workers' health and safety;
- help the company fulfil any obligations established by the competent authority; and
- cooperate with the company on the prevention of accidents and the minimization of harmful consequences.

13.5. Specific Standards

The Law for the Prevention of Occupational Hazards obliges companies to provide employees with adequate clothing and equipment to prevent injuries and guarantee employees' safety. Depending on the activities, the preventive services may determine the relevant equipment to be provided.

This clothing must be adequately renewed, and companies must keep a record of the clothing and equipment delivered to each employee.

13.6. Injury or Accident at Work

Employers must complete an official accident report form whenever an employee is absent from work for one or more days due to an accident (other than the day of the accident itself). They must file the form with the body in charge of industrial accident and illness benefits (the National Institute of Social Security or Social Security's Industrial Accident Mutual).

If more than four employees are affected, or if an employee has died, the company must send an official notice to the labour authorities (either the province's or the Autonomous Community's) within twenty-four hours of the accident. The Labour Authority will notify the Labour Inspector, who will then prepare a report on the incident after investigating the accident.

All employers also must keep a monthly record of all industrial accidents that do not result in time off on medical grounds and submit it to the Social Security services competent body, together with a monthly list of those absent (or dead) due to industrial accidents.

13.7. Workplace Violence

Violence in the workplace is uncommon in Spain. However, any kind of violence in the workplace is prohibited, and it falls on the employer to adopt the necessary measures to avoid workplace violence as part of its obligations.

Organic Law 10/2022, of 6 September, on the comprehensive guarantee of sexual liberty, establishes that all companies should promote working conditions that prevent the commission of crimes and other conduct against sexual freedom and moral integrity at work, with special emphasis on sexual harassment and harassment based on sex.

Likewise, companies shall establish specific procedures for the prevention of such conduct and to channel any complaints or claims that may be made by the victims, including specifically those suffered in the digital sphere.

Measures to be negotiated with workers' representatives may be established, such as the drafting and dissemination of codes of good practice, information campaigns, action protocols or training actions.

Awareness and offer training for the integral protection against sexual violence to all personnel in their service shall be promoted.

Companies shall include sexual violence among the concurrent occupational risks in the risk assessment of the different jobs occupied by female workers and shall train and inform their female workers accordingly.

Companies should introduce a code of conduct that defines behaviour that is considered disruptive or violent and establish a procedure for investigating alleged violations of the code of conduct. The company should also adopt a disciplinary procedure for violent acts. In such cases, a disciplinary dismissal would be an adequate response.

13.8. Fines and Penalties

Infringements of the Law for the Prevention of Occupational Hazards are penalized strictly and severely with fines of up to EUR 983,736 in extremely severe circumstances (very serious infringements). However, most infringements are serious infringements (with fines ranging from EUR 2,451 to EUR 49,180). The *Real Decreto Legislativo 5/2000*, of 4 August, of infractions and penalties in labour relations establishes the list of possible infractions of all in sections 11–13 and their corresponding penalties.

If any company's infringement of health and safety legal provisions is deemed the cause of any work accident in any of the companies' workplaces, the company may have to compensate the employee for damages due to criminal and/or civil liability.

If the accident results in payment of a public pension (disability, widows, or orphans), the company could be required to pay the employee or the employee's relatives an additional amount, calculated as a percentage of the social security benefits (ranging from 30% to 50%).

Under the Law for the Prevention of Occupational Hazards, the Labour and Social Security Inspector plays an important role in supervising and monitoring occupational health and safety measures. The Inspector has the authority to require employers to remedy any breaches of the regulations on the prevention of occupational risks and to order the immediate cessation of work if the breach gives rise to serious and imminent danger to employees' health and safety at work.

13.9. Checklist of Do's and Don'ts

- Strictly comply with all health and safety obligations and designate one person in the company to oversee compliance.
- Take health and safety in the workplace seriously, do not allow for any unsafe employment behaviour and impose disciplinary measures quickly and effectively. Make it clear that unsafe behaviour will not be tolerated.
- Keep all the required documents and information, such as risk evaluations, safety plans and procedures, updated and well organized, and make sure the person responsible for health and safety is familiar with them and able to manage them promptly and accurately.
- In the event of an accident, immediately call for legal counsel since it is crucial in the first twenty-four–forty-eight hours after the accident when the first investigations take place.

14. GENERAL IMMIGRATION OVERVIEW IN SPAIN

14.1. Overview of Laws Controlling Immigration

EU nationals, citizens of the European Economic Area (EEA) and Switzerland[32] are entitled to live and work in Spain without any restrictions and without obtaining a residence and work permit; they are required to only fulfil certain formalities.

Non-EU nationals of working age who wish to reside and work legally in Spain must obtain an upfront residence and work permit. To obtain a residence and work permit, it is necessary to meet certain requirements and submit, among other documents, a written employment contract or documentary evidence that the foreign national has been offered employment. When applying for the residence and work permit in Spain, the employee needs to prove that: (1) he/she has not overstayed beyond the ninety days in a 180 days period in the *Schengen* area; and (2) he/she has no

32. European Community Treaty; Regulation EEC 1612/68; Dir. 2004/38/EC; *Real Decreto 240/2007*).

criminal record in Spain or in the countries where he/she has resided for the past five years, for criminal offences defined in the relevant Spanish legislation.

The regulatory framework for immigration in Spain is stated in mainly two Laws, the application of which depends on the immigration purpose of the interested parties. Those are classified into two frameworks: *Entrepreneurs Law* (*Law 14/2013, of 27 September, on supporting entrepreneurs* and their internationalization) and *Law on Foreigners* (*LO 4/2000, of 11 January, on the rights and freedoms of foreigners in Spain and their social integration* and its regulation).

Entrepreneurs Law

The Entrepreneurs Act contemplates a wide range of permit possibilities, such as for highly qualified professionals, intra-company transfers, entrepreneurs and investors, and some others, and promotes entrepreneurial culture, attracting foreign talent without taking into account the national employment market, and it offers an accessible entrance of investment and talent beneficial for the region.

The Entrepreneurs Act offers an expedited path to shorten the timing of the process. In this regard, the maximum decision-making period by law will be twenty working days from the filing of the application. If no decision is reached within the said period, the permit will be deemed granted due to administrative silence. Residence permits included in this law will be processed electronically by the Unit for Large Companies and Strategic Economic Sectors.

Also, decisions on visa applications at the relevant Spanish Consulate, when applicable,[33] will be made and notified within a period of ten working days from the date of filing the visa application.

The Entrepreneurs Act also offers residence permits to the dependents of the spouse or person with an analogous affective relationship, children who are minors or those of legal age who, being financially dependent on the holder, have not formed a family unit for themselves and the parents in their charge, who accompany or join the foreign nationals.

A brief description of the main permits under the Entrepreneurs Law is listed below.

33. It is possible to submit the Residence Application through an in-country process while the person is in Spain on tourist/business status (within the ninety days in a 180 days period in the *Schengen* area). The application for residence permits provided in the *Entrepreneurs Law* shall extend the validity of the stay of the applicant in Spain until the application is resolved. Under then, once in receipt of the residence permit, the employee will not need to apply for the Work Visa at the Spanish Consulate, expediting the process.

Investors

If a person has made a significant investment in Spain, he/she can take advantage of the Spanish migration scheme for investors.

For a capital investment to be considered significant, one of the following criteria must be fulfilled:

(a) An initial investment with a value equal to or greater than:
  - EUR 2 million in Spanish public debt securities.
  - EUR 1 million in shares or equity investments in Spanish capital companies with a real estate business activity; in investment funds, closed-end investment funds or venture capital funds; or in bank deposits in Spanish financial institutions.

(b) The *acquisition of real estate property in Spain* with an investment value equal to or greater than EUR 500,000 per applicant, free of all liens or encumbrances.

(c) A *business project intended to be carried out in Spain that is deemed and proved to be of general interest*, being necessary to be considered as such the fulfilment of at least one of the following conditions:
  - the creation of jobs;
  - making an investment with relevant socio-economic impact in the geographic area where the activity will be carried out;
  - a relevant contribution to scientific and/or technological innovation.

There are two options:

(i) An *investor visa*, if the applicant is outside of Spain when the application is submitted.

(ii) A *residence permit* if the applicant is currently in Spain under legal status when submitting the application.

Duration: Visa: one year. Initial residence permit: two years. Renewal of the residence permit: five years, provided that the conditions are maintained.

Renewal does not require *effective* residence in Spain.

Entrepreneurs and Business Activity

Foreign nationals willing to start up an innovative business of particular economic interest in Spain can take advantage of the Spanish migration scheme for entrepreneurs.

There are two options:

(1) A *start-up visa* if the applicant is outside of Spain and he/she needs to come to Spain to make the necessary preparatory arrangements to be able to develop an enterprising activity.

(2) A *residence permit* if the applicant is currently in Spain and can set up the business. The visa holders referred to in the preceding paragraph will be eligible for entrepreneurial residence status without the need to apply for a visa. There is no need for the residence permit applicant to remain in Spain for a minimum period of time when it can be proved that the business activity for which the visa was applied has effectively been started.

There are neither minimum capital requirements nor minimum number of jobs to create.

The Spanish system is based on a case-by-case analysis. For this reason, business plans are required to know if the activity has a special economic interest for Spain or not.

Duration: Visa: one year. Initial residence permit: two years. Renewal of the residence permit: other two years.

Highly Qualified Professionals

Companies needing to incorporate into Spanish territory foreign professionals to perform an employment or professional relationship covered under any of the following cases may apply for a residence permit for highly qualified professionals, which will be valid throughout Spain:

(a) Management or highly qualified personnel when the company or group of companies meet one of the following characteristics:
   - Average workforce during the three months immediately prior to the filing of the application greater than two hundred and fifty workers in Spain, registered in the relevant Social Security system.
   - Annual net business turnover in Spain of over EUR 50 million or volume of own funds or equity or net worth in Spain exceeding EUR 43 million.
   - Annual average gross investment from abroad, not less than EUR 1 million in the three years immediately prior to the application filing date.
   - Companies with an investment stock value or position, according to the latest data from the Foreign Investments Registry of the Ministry of Economy and Competitiveness of over EUR 3 million.
   - In the case of small- and medium-sized businesses established in Spain, they belong to a sector considered strategic, which is certified by a report from the relevant authority.

(b) Management or highly qualified personnel forming part of a *business project* involving one or several of the following conditions:
   - A significant increase in the creation of direct jobs by the company requesting recruitment.
   - Maintenance of employment.

- A significant increase in the creation of jobs in the business sector or geographic area where the professional activity is to be performed.
- An extraordinary investment with a relevant social and economic impact in the geographic area where the professional activity is to be performed.
- The concurrence of reasons of interest for Spain's commercial and investment policy.
- A relevant contribution to scientific and/or technological innovation.

(c) This category will be certified by the corresponding report issued by the relevant Spanish Authority.
(d) Graduates and postgraduates from renowned prestigious universities and business schools.

Under the Highly Qualified Work Permit, the employee will be hired directly by the Spanish Company.

Duration: Initial residence permit: three years. Renewal of the residence permit: another two years, as long as the requirements have been fulfilled.

Intra-Company Transfer

Those foreign nationals who are posted to Spain within the framework of an employment or professional relationship or for professional training purposes with a company or group of companies established in Spain or in another country must hold the relevant permit in accordance with the duration of their posting which will be valid throughout the national territory.

Under this category of a permit, the employee will maintain his labour relationship with the origin company abroad while his assignment is in Spain.

The transfer can be between companies that belong to the same group or between different companies. In the latter, it will be based on a Service Agreement signed by the different companies.

The following requirements must be met:

(a) The existence of an actual business activity and, where applicable, that of the business group.
(b) Higher education qualification or equivalent or, where applicable, a minimum professional experience of three years in the same area.
(c) The existence of a previous and continuous employment or professional relationship of three months with one or more of the companies of the group.
(d) Company documentation accrediting the posting.

There are two types of residence permits for Intra-corporate Transfers (ICTs):

(i) EU ICT work permit: This permit is issued in the case of temporary postings to work as a manager, specialist or for training purposes from a company established outside the EU to the same company or group of companies established in Spain or to a different company based on the Service Agreement signed by them.

(ii) National residence permit for ICTs: This permit shall be applicable in the cases not included in the paragraph above. It also applies when the EU ICT Intra-company duration has reached the maximum period of time allowed.

Duration: Initial National ICT Permit: two years. Residence permits can be renewed for an additional two-year period as long as the conditions and requirements have been fulfilled.

ICT EU – Managers and specialists: three years. Trainee employees: one year.

Important Note

Foreign nationals must continue to meet, during the visas or permit periods of validity, the conditions under which these had been granted.

Any modification during the residence that affects the admission conditions shall be notified by the interested party to the Unit of Large Companies and Strategic Economic Sectors Unit within a thirty-day period.

Organic Law 4/2000

Outside the scheme of the Entrepreneurs Act previously explained, it will be necessary to fulfil the requirements stated in the *Organic Law 4/2000, of 11 January, on the rights and freedoms of foreigners in Spain and their social integration* and its regulation in order to hire non-EU nationals in Spain.

In this regard, the national labour market situation must allow the hiring of foreign non-EU workers, either because the occupation is included in the quarterly National Occupation Shortage List of activities (which are difficult to cover depending on each province in Spain) or by obtaining a certificate issued by the Regional Public Employment Service certifying that there are not legal residents in Spain who can be suitable to cover the job position offered.

Regardless of the above, there are certain situations which are exempted from facing the Spanish labour market test. Some of these situations are the following:

– Chile and Peru nationals.

- Executive roles with broad Power of Attorney to represent the Spanish entity built on trust.
- Spouses and children of working age of those residents in Spain who have previously renewed their residence and work permit.
- Being a child or grandchild of Spanish by birth.
- Non-EU nationals who have Spanish dependents or descendants.
- Investors, teachers, researchers, artists, etc., whose professional activity involves economic, social or labour interest.
- Employees in a workforce of a company or group of companies in another country who intend to develop their work activity for the same company or group in Spain, provided that employee performance requires direct and reliable knowledge of the company.
- Workers needed for the assembly of a productive installation or equipment renovation.

The company will not be able to initiate the labour relationship until the employee is authorized to work in Spain.

14.2. Obligation of the Employer to Comply with the Spanish Regulations

When hiring foreign employees, companies must check that the foreign employees have the appropriate permits. They must not hire employees without a permit or employees with a permit that is inadequate for the company's activity. In addition, the employee needs to have the titles or qualifications required to exercise the profession in Spain.

The employer must be up to date with Spanish social security and tax payments. The employer must comply with Spanish labour laws. In this regard, the employer must fulfil, when applicable, Law 45/1999, of 29 November, *on the posting of workers in the framework of the transnational provision of services.*

14.3. Fines and Penalties

The hiring of non-EEA citizens without a relevant work permit or renewal is considered a very serious infringement, and it results in severe fines. Additionally, the foreign employee could be deported.

14.4. Secondment/Foreign Assignment

Spanish labour regulations also apply to those Spanish employees who are hired by Spanish companies and need to provide services in a foreign country, besides those provisions pertaining to the law enforcement regulations of the country where services are rendered:

Elaborated by the Global Mobility Department at Gesdocument				
www.gdglobalmobility.com	www.gesdocument.com	Facebook	Twitter	LinkedIn

15. RESTRICTIVE COVENANTS AND PROTECTION OF TRADE SECRETS AND CONFIDENTIAL INFORMATION

15.1. Overview

Under Spanish law, labour relationships are governed by the principle of good faith (bona fide). The good faith obligation applies to both the employer and the employee. For example, an employee breaches the duty of good faith if he or she competes against the employer during the employment relationship, solicits employees away from the employer, or talks negatively about the employer and damages its reputation. The employer violates its good faith obligations if it purposely undermines the employee's self-esteem or self-worth by giving him tasks below his professional capabilities or continuously delays the payment of the salaries, as set forth in the Workers' Statute and by Spain's abundant case law.

However, the duty of good faith only applies during the employment relationship. If the employer wants to impose non-compete obligations or protect trade secrets after the termination of employment, it is crucial to establish these post-termination obligations in the employment contract.

15.2. The Law of Trade Secrets

Among the obligations of employees, there is the general obligation of confidentiality as established in our civil and commercial code when requiring good faith in the actions of contracting parties.

In practice, whenever employers want to impose the obligation of confidentiality, specific provisions to prohibit the disclosure of trade secrets are included in the contracts.

Besides company secrets relative to confidential strategies and planning, in Spain, trade secrets are covered by several regulations:

- Inventions and Models. Law 24/2015, of inventions and utility models.
- Distinctive Signs. Law 17/2001, of trademarks.
- Industrial Designs. Law 20/2003, of legal protection of industrial designs.
- Corporate Secrets, Law 1/2019, protection of corporate secrets from employees and ex-employees, which makes it advisable for companies to include confidentiality clauses and limitations in the employment contract in order to control the revelation of sensitive information by employees and ex-employees.

15.2.1. Restrictive Covenants and Non-compete Agreements

Probably the most significant of the restrictive covenants is the non-compete covenant.

The non-compete obligation during the employment relationship is one of the basic characteristics of the employment relationship, and it is part of the good faith principle.

Section 21 of the Workers' Statute allows for post-contractual non-competition obligations for a maximum term of two years after the employment ends. This is subject to the employee receiving adequate economic compensation (a percentage of the remuneration of the employee). It is also subject to the employer having a business interest in preventing the employee from competing.

The covenant can restrict the competition to a certain activity, certain companies, or a geographic area or prohibit any kind of professional activity. The scope of the restrictions set on the future activity of the employee will influence the amount of compensation: the wider the restriction, the larger the amount.

Compensation for restrictive covenants can be paid during the term of the employment relationship, at the time of termination or during the period that the restrictions apply post-termination. The parties can agree to compensation paid in instalments.

However, it is difficult to enforce non-competition obligations under Spanish law because it is often hard to prove the employees' breach.

To obtain adequate compensation in case of a breach of the employee's obligation, it is advisable to contractually establish the consequences of the employee's breach. For example, damages could include a refund of all the amounts paid by the company for the non-compete, plus a penalty of a certain amount, and the actual damages which may result from the employee's competence.

If the employer wishes to restrict the employee from soliciting the employer's customers or employees after the termination of employment, such provision must be included in the post-contractual, non-competition agreement.

Employment contracts can also include covenants to assign the employer the rights to inventions and intellectual property developed with company resources.

15.3. Checklist of Do's and Don'ts

- Non-compete agreements should clearly specify the functional, geographical and temporal scope of the restriction. The limitation of these areas will help establish adequate compensation.
- It is important to sufficiently quantify the amount of compensation to be given to the employee, as if it is not enough, the non-compete covenant will not be valid.
- Include updated confidentiality and limitations in employment contracts.

16. PROTECTION OF WHISTLEBLOWING CLAIMS

16.1. Overview

Whistleblowing in Spain has been regulated by Law 2/2023, of 20 February, regulating the protection of persons who report regulatory infringements and the fight against corruption, transposing Directive (EU) 2019/1937 on the protection of persons who report breaches of Union law.

The regulation aims to facilitate the disclosure of information on breaches in companies, which must provide reporting channels and effective whistleblower protection and make employees aware of the reporting system.

In consequence, companies with more than fifty employees are obliged to establish an internal reporting channel in order to receive information and reports regarding breaches of EU law and serious and very serious criminal and administrative offences.

The Law protects whistleblowers, specifically workers, self-employed persons, shareholders, board members, persons in managerial or supervisory bodies, contractors, subcontractors and suppliers, regardless of whether the relationship has ended or has yet to begin, and even volunteers, interns, and paid or unpaid trainees. Besides whistleblowers, natural persons who assist a whistleblower in the reporting process in a work-related context; natural persons connected to the whistleblower and who may suffer retaliation, such as colleagues or relatives of the whistleblower; and legal entities that the whistleblower works for or is otherwise connected within a work-related context, or in which the whistleblower holds a significant stake are also protected.

To benefit from the special protection, the information or reporting must be provided honestly and in good faith; there must be reasonable cause to believe the veracity of the alleged breach, and it must be within the Law's scope of protection.

Whistleblowers will be protected for two years from any form of retaliation for disclosing information. If the whistleblower reasonably proves that, having reported or publicly disclosed a breach, they have suffered a detriment, it will be presumed in legal proceedings that the detriment was made in retaliation, and the burden of proof will shift to the person who took the detrimental action, who should then demonstrate that the action taken was not linked in any way to the reporting or the public disclosure.

Acts of retaliation will be declared null and will result in disciplinary or liability measures, including compensation for damages.

Whistleblowers, including workers' legal representatives, will not be considered to have breached any restriction on disclosure of information in respect of their report, provided that there are reasonable grounds to believe that the reporting or public disclosure of that information was necessary.

The Law establishes a penalty system, imposing fines on individuals and companies for committing offences defined as such. The breach of the obligation to have an internal reporting system and acts of retaliation against whistleblowers are punishable with fines ranging between EUR 30,001 and EUR 300,000 for individuals and EUR 600,001 and EUR 1,000,000 for companies. It lays down additional penalties, such as reprimands, a ban on subsidies and other tax advantages for four years, and a three-year ban on entering into contracts with public sector entities.

16.1.1. Good Governance

The Special Working Group on the Good Governance of Listed Companies of the Spanish Government's Report of Recommendations for Spanish Listed Companies recommended that companies establish a '*whistleblowing*' procedure under the supervision of the auditors' commission. Under this procedure, employees can confidentially or even anonymously report any possible illegalities they observe in the company's conduct. The Working Group believes that the cases dealt with will mainly refer to financial or accounting matters, and companies establishing such mechanisms will do so in strict adherence to the terms of data protection legislation.

16.1.2. Data Protection

Any whistleblowing protection procedure must comply with the provisions set out in the new above-mentioned LOPDGDD and in the GDPR. The LOPDGDD establishes that it is lawful, subject to the conditions and guarantees established by section 24 of the LOPDGDD, to develop and maintain information systems to report, even anonymously, the commission on unlawful acts or behaviour within companies or by third parties that use their services.

According to section 24 of the LOPDGDD, access to the data obtained from internal whistleblowing systems is to be restricted exclusively to those persons performing internal control and compliance duties or to the data processors specifically designated. Third-party access may be allowed on an exceptional basis when it is necessary to take disciplinary action or carry out pertinent legal proceedings. In this regard, access to human resources personnel is only permitted when it may be necessary to take disciplinary measures against an employee.

As regards the retention period, the personal data can only be maintained for as long as it is necessary to determine whether there are grounds to initiate an investigation of the reported facts. In any event, personal data must be removed from the system after three months from its inclusion unless it is necessary to retain it for compliance purposes. Once the three-month term has been exceeded, personal data may continue to be used for disciplinary purposes to investigate the matters that have been reported, although the data must not be held on the whistleblowing system.

Additionally, the Spanish Data Protection Agency (SDPA) has advised that prior to the enactment of a whistleblowing scheme, the company should inform all employees of: (i) conducts that could be denounced; (ii) the system for filing complaints under the scheme; (iii) the personal data to be provided by the complainant when filing the complaint; (iv) the likely measures to be adopted in case of being accused – including a description of the investigation proceedings and set of sanctions associated with the whistleblowing scheme; and (v) the proceedings and means made available to employees to access, amend, oppose or have removed their personal data associated with an investigation proceeding derived from a complaint filed through the whistleblowing scheme.

In addition to the foregoing, the Whistleblowing Directive states that any processing of personal data carried out considering its provisions must respect the principles included in the GDPR and, accordingly, that personal data shall not be collected unless it is undeniably relevant to the handling of a specific complaint. If such personal data has been collected accidentally, it shall be deleted without undue delay.

Also, the Whistleblowing Directive obliges Member States to ensure that the competent authorities have adequate protection procedures for the handling of complaints and for the protection of the personal data of those mentioned in the complaint (which require their data to be protected at all stages of the procedure).

To finish, it should be in any case noted that according to the Whistleblowing Directive the protection of privacy and personal data is expressly included among the categories or types of offences for which the complaint channels should be available.

16.2. Checklist of Do's and Don'ts

- Establish a whistleblowing procedure which ensures that all information received will be adequately processed and the whistleblowing employee shall not suffer any damaging consequences.
- Take complaints seriously but not alarmingly. The investigation of such issues should be carried out effectively and discreetly.
- Train supervisors to deal with these situations carefully.
- Employers may find it convenient to establish such procedures in order to avoid conflicts within the company to be known outside of it.

17. PROHIBITION OF DISCRIMINATION IN THE WORKPLACE

17.1. Overview of Anti-discrimination Laws

The Spanish Constitution guarantees equal treatment of citizens. Section 14 expressly forbids any kind of discrimination based on birth, race, gender, religion, ideology or any other personal or social circumstance.

Pursuant to section 4 of the Workers' Statute, the labour force in Spain is protected against any kind of direct or indirect discrimination on the grounds of gender, marital status, age, racial or ethnic origin, social circumstances, religious or moral convictions, ideology, sexual orientation, registration or non-registration with a union, language, and disability (if the disabled person can carry out the employment-related services for which that person was hired).

Under section 17 of the Workers' Statute, any legislation, section of a bargaining agreement, individual agreement or employer's unilateral decision that contravenes the protection granted in section 4 of the Workers' Statute will be rendered null and void.

Under section 17 of the Workers' Statute, any legislation, section of a bargaining agreement, individual agreement or employer's unilateral decision that contravenes the protection granted in section 4 of the Workers' Statute will be rendered null and void.

The same remuneration – directly or indirectly and regardless of its nature (whether fixed, variable, salary or in kind) – must be paid for work of equal value, with no gender-based discrimination in any of the remuneration factors or conditions.

Work of the same value as other work is performed when 'the nature of the functions or tasks actually entrusted; the educational, professional, and training conditions required to perform it; the factors strictly related to its performance; and the working conditions in which those activities are actually performed are equivalent.'

Law 15/2022, for equal treatment and non-discrimination, in force since 14 July 2022, extended the scope of protection against discrimination, addressing the causes and potential forms of discrimination.

It is introduced as factors of discrimination, illness, health condition, serological status and genetic predisposition to suffer from pathologies and disorders, as well as gender expression, language and socioeconomic situation. Therefore, those factors are no longer required to be linked to a disability or a long-term illness to be considered discriminatory.

It forbids employers from asking job applicants about their health conditions.

As regards forms of discrimination, as well as direct and indirect discrimination, it included the following types:

- Discrimination by error: based on incorrect consideration of the characteristics of the person or persons discriminated against.
- Multiple discrimination: discrimination against one person on the basis of more than one ground.
- Intersectional discrimination: when several grounds operate simultaneously and interact in an inseparable manner, producing a distinct form of discrimination.
- The definition of indirect discrimination is extended and includes cases where the result could be harmful, although not necessarily so.

Discrimination also refers to denial of reasonable accommodation, harassment, incitement, order or instruction to discriminate or to commit an act of intolerance, reprisals or non-compliance with positive action, inaction, neglect of duties or breach of duties.

Section 8 of the Law Infractions and Sanction of Employment and Social Security obligations (*Real Decreto Legislativo 5/2000*, of 4 August) sanctions as very serious infractions all unilateral decisions by the employer that:

- discriminate, either directly or indirectly, based on age or disability in matters relative to remuneration, working time, training, promotion or other working conditions;
- discriminate based on gender, origin (either racial or ethnic), marital status, social condition, religion or beliefs, political ideas, sexual orientation, membership to trade unions or lack of it, family relationship to other employees within the company, or use of another of the languages existing in Spain; or
- retaliate against an employee for any discrimination complaint made by the employee or any equal protection claim, charge, grievance or lawsuit brought before the courts or the administrative authorities.

Harassment based on racial or ethnic origin, religion or convictions, disability, age and sexual orientation and sexual harassment are also very serious infractions of the employment obligations when they take place within the scope of the managerial powers of the company, that is, in connection with the employment relationship, regardless of the person doing the harassment. Harassment by another employee is also a violation if the employer is aware of the harassment and has not adopted the measures necessary to stop it.

The sanction for these infractions is a fine ranging from EUR 7,501 to EUR 225,018.

17.2. Age Discrimination

During recruitment, Spanish labour regulations prohibit discrimination based on age. While Article 17 of the Workers' Statute provides that there will be no discrimination based on age, there are a number of measures aimed at promoting the employment of individuals under 30 and over 45 years of age.

17.3. Race Discrimination

A company cannot discriminate against an employee based on nationality, ethnic or national origin, race, or any other racial circumstance. Racially discriminatory decisions are null and void.

In Spain, there is no affirmative action expressly allowed in this area, although it would be admitted in the application of EU Directives. However, race discrimination is not currently an issue in employment relationships.

17.4. Sex Discrimination/Sexual Harassment

Spanish labour laws protect employees against behaviour that may attack their dignity or create an intimidating, humiliating and offensive environment because of their gender.[34]

The Workers' Statute explicitly prohibits discrimination based on gender and asserts the employee's right not to be discriminated against on such grounds, either in the hiring process or once employment is secured. The Workers' Statute stipulates that job definition and promotion must be in accordance with regulations that are equally applicable to employees of both sexes.

The Workers' Statute further establishes that where work of equal value is carried out, salaries must be set and paid without any discrimination based on gender. This concept refers not only to equal pay for the same tasks but also to equal pay for different tasks if they have equal value. Objective or neutral criteria must be used in making such an evaluation. For example, criteria such as physical or muscular strength, which would favour men, should not be used.

If the employee's gender is a necessary characteristic of the position to be filled (e.g., a woman playing a female role in a play), it is lawful to discriminate between the sexes.

The Gender Equality Law (*Ley Orgánica para la Igualdad Efectiva entre Mujeres y Hombres 3/2007*, of 22 March) prohibits gender discrimination in the workplace and also in a number of other environments such as universities, public administration, media and armed forces.

The objectives of this law are to:

- effectively achieve equal treatment and equal opportunity between men and women;
- eliminate any kind of discrimination against women.

17.4.1. Relevant Concepts of the Law

The law defines several concepts which are relevant for the understanding of the measures adopted therein, as follows:

> Equal treatment of men and women. This principle implies the absence of all discrimination, direct or indirect, based on gender, and especially those derived from maternity, assumption of family obligations and marital status.

34. Spanish Constitution (s. 14); Workers' Statute (s. 17), and the Law for Gender Equality.

> In the employment area, equal treatment applies to several issues: employment access, professional training and promotion, working conditions (especially remuneration conditions), affiliation and participation in trade unions....

Discrimination, which can be either direct or indirect:

- *Direct discrimination*: when someone is treated, because of their gender, in a less favourable way than others in comparable situations.
- *Indirect discrimination*: This happens when a disposition, criteria or practice are apparently neutral but, in fact, places persons of a certain gender at a disadvantage.

For example, Spain's Constitutional Court described such a situation in a decision 250/2000, of 30 October. It was a case involving the remuneration established in a collective agreement for the citric sector in a specific region of Spain. There were two different professional categories, one of which had lower remuneration, although the work carried out in both categories was of equal value. The lower remuneration category was mainly composed of women, and the other category was composed of men. The Constitutional Court deemed this an indirect discrimination.

The law expressly establishes that, exceptionally, those practices, dispositions or criteria which may be objectively justified to obtain a legitimate objective shall not be considered indirect discrimination.

The Gender Equality Law obliges companies to promote work conditions that avoid sexual and gender-based harassment. Companies must establish specific procedures to prevent harassment and provide victims with an opportunity to file grievances and claims.

The definition of professional groups – reserved to collective bargaining – must comply with criteria and systems that, based on a correlative analysis of biased gender, work positions, and the criteria for assignment and remuneration, are intended to guarantee the absence of any direct or indirect discrimination against women or men. These criteria and systems must establish the same remuneration for work of equal value.

Companies with at least fifty employees that detect that the average remuneration of employees of either gender is higher than that of the other gender by 25% or more – considering all salaries or the average salary paid – must explicitly justify in the salary registry (defined in question 11) why that gap is not due to reasons related to the employees' gender.

Companies should enact specific codes of conduct, promote information campaigns and train employees and managers to detect and prevent sexual harassment.

17.4.2. Equality Plans

The Gender Equality law establishes certain measures to reinforce and ensure the right to equality and no discrimination between men and women.

These measures can be summed up into the 'planning of equality' in the company. This is the instrumentation within the company of a series of mechanisms to reinforce and guarantee the efficacy of the principle of equal treatment between men and women and the non-discrimination, direct or indirect, based on gender.

This equality planning does not intend to achieve equality by parity criteria, intends to identify situations or potential situations where the principle of equality may be violated, and then establishes measures for the correction or suppression of those situations.

17.4.3. How Should the Planning of Equality Be Done?

Positive action measures are permitted to be introduced in the company through collective bargaining. Also, companies are obliged to negotiate (but not necessarily resolve) potential corrective measures in discriminatory situations. If the parties agree, the negotiation can result in the implementation of a positive action plan. Further, in some cases, the company has an obligation to establish an Equality Plan.

Companies with over fifty employees must prepare and apply an Equality Plan in line with the Gender Equality Law after negotiating, as the case may be, with the employees' legal representatives.

An Equality Plan diagnosis must be carried out – negotiated, as the case may be, with the employees' legal representatives – and must include assessable measures aimed at removing the obstacles that hinder effective equality, at least in the following areas:

- Selection and recruitment process.
- Professional classification.
- Training.
- Promotion.
- Work conditions, including the auditing of women's and men's salaries, including remote working.
- Co-responsible exercise of the rights to a personal, family, and work life.
- Women's underrepresentation.
- Remuneration.
- Prevention of sexual and gender-based harassment.

All companies – regardless of their size – must register their Equality Plan with the new Companies' Equality Plan Registry.

17.4.4. Compliance and Potential Sanctions

Non-compliance with the obligation to establish an Equality Plan will be considered a serious infraction, with fines from EUR 751 to EUR 7,500. The infraction is 'failure to comply with the obligations related to Equality Plans established in the Workers' Statute or in the collective bargaining agreement'.

Not elaborating on an Equality Plan when one should have been imposed as a substitution for fines for discrimination is a very serious infraction, with a fine ranging from EUR 7,501 up to EUR 225,018. Besides these sanctions, the employer will also be subject to the fines which the Equality Plan was meant to substitute.

Sexual harassment occurring within the scope of management of the company, regardless of the person doing the harassment, is considered a very serious infraction. The employer can be fined with a penalty ranging from EUR 7,501 up to EUR 225,018.

17.5. Handicap and Disability Discrimination

17.5.1. Pre-existing Illness or Injury

In companies employing more than fifty workers, 2% of the workforce must be persons with disabilities. If the employer cannot find persons with disabilities capable of performing the job, special regulations provide certain alternative measures, which consist of hiring the services or giving occupation to centres of special employment as purveyors or renderers of services for an amount equal to the triple of the annual *Indicador Público de Renta de Efectos Múltiples* (IPREM), set at EUR 600.00 per month) for each disabled employee not hired until 2% of the workforce is reached. It is also valid to give monetary donations and sponsorship to carry activities for the insertion in the job market and job creation to disabled persons, through foundations. Financing Special Olympic activities is also accepted. In this case, the amount shall be at least 1.5 times the annual IPREM for each disabled employee not hired below the 2% quota.

17.5.2. Post-employment Illness or Injury

The same basic provisions of the Spanish Constitution and the Workers' Statute as described above apply to discrimination based on disability. Any action an employer takes against an employee that is directly or indirectly discriminatory on the grounds of disability will be null and void.

The Law for the Prevention of Occupational Hazards requires the employer to adapt the job to the employee's personal circumstances. On that basis, employees should not be hired for jobs where their recognized physical, mental, or sensory disabilities place them, their colleagues or third parties in danger.

In addition to making the job suitable for the employee, the workstation and the workplace also must be suitable. Employers must ensure that the workplace is handicapped-accessible. If the company did not take reasonable steps to adapt to the workplace, the court may hold a dismissal of an employee with disabilities to be unfair and/or ineffective, except in the case of employee misconduct that determines the fairness of the termination. Reasonableness is an issue to be determined according to the merits of each case. Public institutions may subsidize the adaptation of the workplace.

17.5.3. Rights of Employees

Employees can claim against the company if their fundamental civil right is attacked by employers, using specific judicial procedures in which the public attorney protects any public interest that could arise in this procedure.

If an employee files a discrimination claim in the courts, the employee only has to demonstrate that the employer's behaviour could have been discriminatory. The burden then shifts to the employer to prove that their actions were not discriminatory. If the employer is not able to refute the alleged discrimination, the employer shall have to stop all discriminatory behaviour, and moral damages will be awarded to the employee.

17.6. National Origin Discrimination

Section 14 of the Constitution prohibits discrimination based on birth, so an employer cannot discriminate against an employee based on the place where the employee was born.

As stated above regarding immigration policies, in general, and specifically regarding employment issues, foreign employees are entitled to the same rights as national employees.

Employers are strictly forbidden from differentiating between two employees in terms of wages, work hours, place of work, professional category, or any other conditions for national origin reasons.

17.7. Religious Discrimination

Spain is a non-denominational state, and any discrimination connected with personal beliefs (or lack of beliefs) is forbidden in the workplace. Workers cannot, under any circumstance, be obliged to reveal information about their religious beliefs.

17.8. Military Status Discrimination

Armed forces are outside the scope of the application of employment law, and there is no mandatory military service in Spain, so it is not material for the employment relationship.

17.9. Pregnancy Discrimination

Pregnant employees are protected against discrimination, and any measures adopted against them based on their condition will automatically be considered null and void unless there are other legitimate reasons for the measures.

This protection of pregnant employees goes beyond protection against discrimination. The Constitutional Court holds that the termination based on insufficient objective reasons of an employee who was pregnant at the time of termination was declared null and void instead of unfair because of the insufficiency of the reasons, even though the employer was unaware of the employee's condition. The Constitutional Court expressly acknowledged there was no discrimination, but it still declared the termination null and void because the termination of a pregnant employee is null and void unless declared fair by a judge, that is, that the causes for the termination, whether objective or disciplinary are true and sufficient to terminate the relationship.

17.10. Marital Status Discrimination

This is an uncommon issue in Spanish labour relationships.

However, marital status is considered personal information that cannot be required of the employee by the employer, and discrimination based on marital status is expressly in section 4 of the Workers' Statute. The Constitution prohibits discrimination based on any social or personal circumstance.

17.11. Sexual Orientation Discrimination

Sexual orientation is personal and private information that does not need to be given to the employer. Employees can complain against company decisions that could be based on sexual orientation discrimination, based on section 14 of the Constitution and section 4 of the Workers' Statute.

17.12. Retaliation

Section 24 of the Constitution guarantees effective protection from courts and tribunals. This protection has been extended to include protection against any kind of retaliation from employers against employees because they sue the company or make any other complaint, charge, grievance or accusation before any administrative authorities. Any decisions adopted that could be considered directly or indirectly connected with a claim by the employee will also be null and void.

Whistleblowers are specifically protected by Directive 2019/1937 and Law 2/2023, relating to protection against reprisals for people who report violations.

Retaliation is a very serious infraction of the employer's obligations, and it is subject to a fine ranging from EUR 7,501 up to EUR 225,018.

17.13. Constructive Discharge

The term 'constructive discharge' in Spain describes a situation in which an employee is entitled to terminate the employment relationship because the employer breaches its obligations. Such non-compliance constitutes a breach of contract and entitles the employee to terminate employment and to receive the severance compensation established for unfair dismissal. This severance compensation is the same as for unfair dismissal (forty-five calendar days' salary per year of service for the time worked before February 2012, up to forty-two monthly instalments, and thirty-three calendar days' salary per year of service for the time worked after up to twenty-four monthly instalments).

Pursuant to section 50 of the Workers' Statute, an employee can terminate employment for any of the following reasons:

- Substantial modifications to the employment conditions which result in damages to the employee's professional development and are detrimental to his dignity.
- Lack of payment of salaries or continued delay in their payment.

- Any other serious and grave non-compliance by the employer, except in cases of major force. For example, if the company's offices have been flooded and employees are not allowed to work, the employee does not have the right to terminate employment.
- Employer's refusal to reinstate the employee in the former working conditions when a judge declares the substantial modifications of the employment contract enforced by the employer to be unjustified.

A typical example of a cause for constructive discharge is when an employer refuses to give employees any work or gives them work that is demeaning. Even if the employee is still being paid, the employee is entitled to terminate the employment relationship.

In order to prosper, constructive discharge claims must be brought to the industrial courts, and during the procedure, the employee is obliged to continue to work unless it is considered that continuing the work implies an excessive sacrifice for the employee.[35] If the employee proves the employer's serious incompliance, the judge will declare the employment contract to be terminated. The date of termination will be the date of the judicial decision, and the employee's severance compensation will have to be calculated on that date.

17.14. Checklist of Do's and Don'ts

- Always document and prove that reasons for measures are totally unrelated to the employee's situation.
- Establish a code of conduct regarding the avoidance of harassment. Do not allow sexual harassment or even sexually charged jokes in the workplace. Discipline any employees who do not comply with these policies. Fully investigate any situations that may arise.
- When possible, train managers and all other employees to respect diverse beliefs, customs, nationality and any other cultural differences.
- Train managers to recognize and address instances of sexual harassment.

18. SMOKING IN THE WORKPLACE

18.1. Overview of Laws and Regulations in Spain

Smoking is banned in all workplaces.[36] Applicable to any people who are in the workplace: all employees, clients, suppliers or any other people that

35. Supreme Court Decision of 20 Jul. 2012.
36. Law 28/2005 regulating the sale, use and promotion of tobacco products.

could have access to the work centre, regardless of whether access takes place during or outside the employees' work hours.

However, there are exceptions to this general ban. It is permissible to smoke in company cars and in the workplace's outdoor areas if the employer expressly allows it.

Law 28/2005 allows for designated smoking areas in airports, hospitals, transport stations, nightclubs, and catering premises, such as pubs or restaurants, with a total area of over 100 square metres. In small catering premises (less than 100 square metres), the business has discretion to allow smoking (which would apply to the whole establishment, without exception).

Although not specifically indicated in the regulation, it is understood that the possibility to assign smoking areas in certain workplaces does not automatically allow employees who work there to smoke during their working time.

Law 28/2005 sets forth a list of sanctions that apply to infringements of the different obligations regarding tobacco use, including sanctions related to infringements of the smoking ban in the workplace:

- Smoking in places where it is expressly forbidden is penalized with fines ranging from EUR 30 to EUR 600.
- Allowing smoking in areas where it is expressly forbidden (i.e., workplaces) is penalized with fines ranging from EUR 601 to EUR 10,000.
- Assigning smoking areas in places where it is not expressly allowed (e.g., workplaces that are not airports, hospitals or catering premises) is also penalized with fines ranging from EUR 601 to EUR 10,000.

18.2. Checklist of Do's and Don'ts

- Inform employees about and post the smoking regulations in the workplace, and advise them of any outdoor areas where smoking is expressly allowed.
- Control tobacco use by employees, initiating disciplinary actions for breach of the company's smoking policy.
- It is not possible to negotiate or agree with the workers' representatives or the workforce to allow smoking areas in the workplace.
- The smoking ban must be applied in the entire workplace, including restaurants or the company's canteens or cafeterias.
- Employers must inform employees that the smoking ban applies to everybody with access to the workplace, including the employers, management teams, clients, suppliers, employees of subcontracting companies or freelancers, without exception.

- The company's smoking policy must indicate whether it is possible for the employees to smoke outside the workplace during working hours (i.e., if 'smoking breaks' are allowed), the length of these breaks, and whether they are considered working time.

19. USE OF DRUGS AND ALCOHOL IN THE WORKPLACE

19.1. Overview of Laws and Regulations in Spain

Spanish labour law does not specifically regulate the use of drugs or alcohol in the workplace. However, employers can regulate such use in the workplace at their sole discretion.

Generally, an employer's request for information on an employee's use of alcohol or drugs may be considered interference with the employee's right to privacy.

However, Spanish labour regulations establish drunkenness or the use of drugs as a valid cause for disciplinary dismissal if it negatively affects the employee's work.

Employers are obliged to protect an employee's health. In practice, some employers offer periodical medical examinations to employees. However: (i) these medical reviews are voluntary for the employees (except for employees who perform certain high-risk activities); and (ii) employers do not have access to their results; they are only informed of the employee's capacity or non-capacity to carry out their work. The employees have to be informed of what they are going to be tested for, even if it is drugs and alcohol, and employees may refuse to have the test.

19.2. Checklist of Do's and Don'ts

- Unless legally required for the work carried out by the employees, employers cannot impose mandatory medical reviews on employees to verify whether they use drugs or alcohol.
- Establish policies prohibiting the use of drugs or alcohol in the workplace and inform employees of the consequences of doing so.

20. AIDS, HIV, SARS, COVID, BLOOD-BORNE PATHOGENS

20.1. Overview of Laws and Regulations in Spain

According to Spanish labour law, employees' illnesses or medical conditions are private if they do not affect the employees' work.

It is not mandatory for any applicant or employee to give the employer information regarding the illness unless it is justified because of the activity the employee will carry out, for example, employees in sanitary professions.

As indicated above, it is possible for employers to carry out medical reviews of employees or potential employees, although the employees' consent is required. If such testing takes place, employers are informed only of the employee's capacity for a specific work position and not of any specific illnesses the employee may have.

The requirement of the employee's consent may be exempted when, according to section 2.1 of the Law for the Prevention of Occupational Hazards, the medical reviews are essential in order to evaluate the effect of the working conditions on employees or to verify whether the health status of the employee may constitute a risk to himself, other employees or any other people related to the company, or whenever it should be thus established in a disposition related to the specific risk protections and especially dangerous activities. This became especially relevant during the COVID-19 crisis because of the danger of contagion.

Any transgression of the employee's privacy will be considered an act contrary to the mandatory respect for privacy and consideration due to employees' dignity, which is a very serious infraction fined between EUR 7,500 to EUR 225,018.

20.2. Checklist of Do's and Don'ts

- Do not investigate employees' health information, as it is protected by their privacy, and any disclosure or unsolicited information is forbidden by our laws, as it will be considered a transgression of the fundamental right to privacy as established in our Constitution.

21. DRESS AND GROOMING REQUIREMENTS

21.1. Overview of Laws and Regulations in Spain

Employees' physical appearance is protected by their constitutional right to personal privacy and to their own image, set forth in section 18 of the Spanish Constitution and the right to respect the personal dignity of every individual.

Some labour regulations allow restrictions on physical appearance. For instance, under the health and safety regulations, an employer can require the employee to wear safety helmets, protective gloves, or any other protection equipment. Moreover, collective bargaining agreements can set forth specific clothing or grooming obligations, depending on the company's activity or the position of certain employees.

In addition, the employer can control employees' physical appearance if it is: (i) justified by the nature of the employment relationship, and (ii) proportional to the aim of the measure.

Thus, if their work implies being in touch with the public or clients of the employee, the employer can require employees to wear a uniform or inform them about the dress or grooming appearance that the employer considers 'adequate'.

For example, a hospital required nurses to wear a uniform that was composed of a skirt, apron and cap. The court (*Tribunal Superior de Justicia de Andalucía, Málaga*, 27 November 2008) decided that the nature of the business and the role of the uniformed nurses justified the obligation to wear the uniform.

If there is no legal provision limiting employees' physical appearance, any interference by employers in employees' physical appearance could be considered a violation of their constitutional right to their own appearance. The appearance requirements could be declared null and void.

21.2. Checklist of Do's and Don'ts

- It is advisable to have a written company policy regulating the physical appearance of employees.
- Any limitation on employees' physical appearance must be justified and proportional to the aim of the measure.
- Clearly state which employees are affected by such company policy and the consequences of non-compliance.

22. PRIVACY, TECHNOLOGY AND TRANSFER OF PERSONAL DATA

22.1. Privacy Rights of Employees

The Spanish Constitution protects each employee's right to privacy. Employers cannot interfere with their employees' right to privacy without serious justification.

Section 18 of the Constitution sets forth a general principle of sanctity of the employee and the employee's locker or any other personal property. The employer is allowed access if it is justified by the company's interest in the protection of its belongings or if it is in the interest of another employee, and only if access is carried out in the work centre, during working time and in the presence of workers' representatives.

The LOPDGDD expressly acknowledges employees' right to the protection of their privacy when using digital devices provided to them by their employer, and it requires companies to establish the criteria for employees' use of those digital devices, respecting in all cases the minimum privacy protection standards, according to the requirements of the European Court of Human Rights (*Barbulescu II* case). The company must inform employees of these criteria, and employees' legal representatives must be involved in establishing these criteria.

Video monitoring of the workplace is permitted if the company has informed the employees and their representatives – if applicable – of this measure in an explicit, clear and concise way. However, the duty to inform will be considered fulfilled when employees are captured committing a flagrantly illegal act, and there is at least the informative sign placed in a sufficiently visible location specifying, at least, that processing may be carried out, the identity of the data controller, and the employees' possibility of exercising their rights under Articles 15–22 of the GDPR. The European Court of Human Rights ruled on 19 October 2019 (*López Ribalda* case), applying *Barbulescu II*, that there was no need to notify of the installation of cameras to supervise the activity of employees (in this case, cashiers at a supermarket) when there were rational suspicions of misdemeanour because of cash discrepancies because the cameras were visible, the installation lasted only ten days, and their recording was viewed by a limited number of people. It is prohibited to instal cameras in employees' rest or recreation areas, such as changing rooms, toilets, dining rooms and similar spaces. As for audio recording in the workplace, it is only allowed on the grounds of ensuring the safety of people, property or facilities. In any case, the company must respect the principle of proportionality and of minimum intervention.

Finally, the company can process the data collected through geolocation systems to monitor its employees' performance. In order to do so, it must inform the employees and their representatives, if applicable, in an explicit, clear and concise way, of the existence and characteristics of these devices, including their rights of access, rectification, erasure, and the right to restriction of the processing. The LOPDGDD does not refer to the purpose of the installation of the device among the points included in the duty of information.

22.2. Checklist of Do's and Don'ts

- Establish a company policy regulating the use of computers, other electronic media, Internet access and work e-mail.

- This policy must inform the employee about what uses of these resources are allowed and should exclude any use for private purposes.
- Employees should be warned periodically that the employer controls and monitors all communications and computer media.
- Make sure employees are aware that fraudulent use of electronic media will result in disciplinary actions.
- Post visible signs and notices warning of video surveillance taking place, even if it is outside a closed building.
- Do not do video monitoring in places where the privacy or dignity of employees may be considered violated, such as restrooms or cafeterias.

23. WORKPLACE INVESTIGATIONS FOR COMPLAINTS OF DISCRIMINATION, HARASSMENT, FRAUD, THEFT AND WHISTLEBLOWING

23.1. Overview of Laws and Regulations in Spain

Collective bargaining agreements applicable to every company may impose certain procedures to investigate infringements prior to initiating disciplinary actions against employees.

Employers can define the investigation process that should be followed in the case of complaints of discrimination, harassment, fraud, theft, and whistleblowing.

As companies are obliged to respect employees' right to equal treatment, it is mandatory that investigation measures avoid any kind of discrimination (specifically between men and women). These measures must be negotiated and agreed upon with the workers' representatives.

23.2. Whistleblowing

Whistleblowing in Spain has been regulated by Law 2/2023, of 20 February, regulating the protection of persons who report regulatory infringements and the fight against corruption, transposing Directive (EU) 2019/1937, on the protection of persons who report breaches of Union law.

The regulation aims to facilitate the disclosure of information on breaches in companies, which must provide reporting channels and effective whistleblower protection and make employees aware of the reporting system.

In consequence, companies with more than fifty employees are obliged to establish an internal reporting channel in order to receive information and reports regarding breaches of EU law and serious and very serious criminal and administrative offences.

As mentioned above in section 16 'Protection of Whistleblowing Claims', the Law protects whistleblowers, specifically workers, self-employed persons, shareholders, board members, persons in managerial or supervisory bodies, contractors, subcontractors and suppliers, regardless of whether the relationship has ended or has yet to begin, and even volunteers, interns, and paid or unpaid trainees. Besides whistleblowers, natural persons who assist a whistleblower in the reporting process in a work-related context; natural persons connected to the whistleblower and who may suffer retaliation, such as colleagues or relatives of the whistleblower; and legal entities that the whistleblower works for or is otherwise connected within a work-related context, or in which the whistleblower holds a significant stake are also protected.

To benefit from the special protection, the information or reporting must be provided honestly and in good faith; there must be reasonable cause to believe the veracity of the alleged breach, and it must be within the Law's scope of protection.

Companies with over 249 employees had until 13 June 2023 to establish the internal reporting channel, while the deadline for those with 50 to 249 employees was 1 December 2023.

Instead of relying on a single reporting channel, informants can provide information on or report breaches and irregularities through any of the following:

- The company's internal channel.
- An external channel or Independent Whistleblower Protection Authority.
- Directly to the public through online platforms or social media, or to the media, among others, when the internal or external channels have been ineffective, there is an imminent danger to the public interest, or there is a risk of retaliation or of the breach not being effectively addressed.

Once information is received, an acknowledgement of receipt must be issued to the reporting person within seven days of providing information on or reporting the breach. The management and investigation of the information or reported facts cannot last longer than three months except in particularly complex cases, where the deadline can be extended by another three months.

Companies must publicize and provide information regarding the use of the internal reporting channel and the key principles of its management procedure. If the company has a website, the channel must appear on the homepage in a separate, easily identifiable section.

A person in charge of the system must be designated, namely a manager appointed by the managerial body, who will perform these duties independently. The company's compliance officer may fill this position.

Companies must register any information they receive and their internal investigations. The register is not public. The content can only be totally or partially accessed if the competent legal authority submits a reasoned request to this effect.

Whistleblowers will be protected for two years from any form of retaliation for disclosing information. If whistleblowers reasonably prove that, having reported or publicly disclosed a breach, they have suffered a detriment, it will be presumed in legal proceedings that the detriment was made in retaliation, and the burden of proof will shift to the person who took the detrimental action, who should then demonstrate that the action taken was not linked in any way to the reporting or the public disclosure.

Acts of retaliation will be declared null and will result in disciplinary or liability measures, including compensation for damages.

Whistleblowers, including workers' legal representatives, will not be considered to have breached any restriction on disclosure of information in respect of their report, provided that there are reasonable grounds to believe that the reporting or public disclosure of that information was necessary.

The Law establishes a penalty system, imposing fines on individuals and companies for committing offences defined as such. The breach of the obligation to have an internal reporting system and acts of retaliation against whistleblowers are punishable with fines ranging between EUR 30,001 and EUR 300,000 for individuals and EUR 600,001 and EUR 1,000,000 for companies. It lays down additional penalties, such as reprimands, a ban on subsidies and other tax advantages for four years, and a three-year ban on entering into contracts with public sector entities.

23.2. Checklist of Do's and Don'ts

Employers must define with the workers' representatives the actions to avoid discrimination or harassment in the workplace, defining which kind of conduct is not allowed in the company.

Employers must consult with the workers' representatives on the procedure to be followed when there are complaints of this nature, specifying: (i) the person responsible for dealing with complaints, (ii) the constitution of an investigating committee, and (iii) the measures to be adopted when there is proof of the complaints, etc.

Make sure all the employees in the company are fully aware and cognizant of the procedures to be followed in case of harassment.

24. AFFIRMATIVE ACTION/NON-DISCRIMINATION REQUIREMENTS

24.1. Overview of Laws and Regulations in Spain

Spanish labour law does not impose a specific diversity requirement, with the exception of the 2% quota of disabled people in companies with more than fifty employees, although it does establish that no employee can be discriminated against based on gender, race, sexual orientation or any other reason.

Provisions for positive action can be found in the Gender Equality Law (*Ley Orgánica 3/2007*, for the Effective Equality of Men and Women), which charges public authorities with the obligation of adopting specific measures in favour of women to correct inequality. Those specific measures will only be applicable during the time the inequality situation should subsist and as long as they are reasonable and proportional to the objective pursued in each case. These measures can also be adopted by private persons when needed.

For example, if only 20% of a bank's branch managers are women, the company may hire women over men. In time, more women will be promoted to manager positions.

The adoption of these measures will, in some cases, result in injustices. In the previous example, female employees will have an unfair advantage over male employees who wish to become managers. These unfair situations are justified by the purpose of the measures, which is to correct an even more unfair situation.

In addition, the Gender Equality Law requires that these measures respect certain limits:

- They may only be used in order to correct evident situations of inequality.
- They must be necessarily limited in time and only as long as the inequality situations subsist.
- The measures must be reasonable and proportional to the circumstances in each case.

Besides, companies with fifty or more employees that identify a pay gap of 25% or more between employees of either gender must provide an objective and reasonable justification for it.

To encourage employers to take action to remedy gender inequality, the Ministry of Work and Immigration grants Distinctives of Equality to companies that stand out because of their application of equality measures. This distinctive may be used in commercial relations and for publicity purposes to enhance the company's reputation.

Companies have to request the Distinctive from the Ministry. To qualify for a Distinctive, they must present a report on the equality measures adopted by the company. The Ministry evaluates:

- equilibrium between the number of men and women in positions of management in the company and in the rest of the professional categories; and
- adoption of Equality Plans and other innovative measures that identify situations or potential situations where the principle of equality may be violated, and then establish measures for the correction or suppression of those situations.

24.2. Checklist of Do's and Don'ts

- Be very strict in the diagnosis of the situation, as it is essential in order to decide on adequate measures to remedy inequality.
- Involve workers' representatives in the equality planning process even beyond what is legally required since it gives transparency and reinforces the intentions of the company.
- Explain to the workforce the Plan and the measures adopted to enforce equality and avoid discrimination.

25. RESOLUTION OF LABOUR, DISCRIMINATION AND EMPLOYMENT DISPUTES: LITIGATION, ARBITRATION, MEDIATION AND CONCILIATION

The applicable law for the resolution of conflicts relative to employment is Law for Social Jurisdiction (*Ley 36/2011*, of 10 October, *reguladora de la Jurisdicción Social*), which establishes that industrial jurisdictional organisms (courts and tribunals) have exclusive jurisdiction over the social or employment branch of the law, both in individual and collective conflicts.

25.1. Internal Dispute Resolution Process

Employers can establish a process for resolving internal disputes as long as it responds to the company's reasonable managerial powers and control of its employees while they are developing their work.

Collective bargaining agreements often include the obligation to conduct a formal hearing when an employee is disciplined. Failure to follow the bargained procedures will result in the disciplinary measure being considered unjustified and, therefore, unfair.

25.2. Mediation and Conciliation

In most cases, the Law for Social Jurisdiction establishes that before filing a labour-related claim with the Spanish labour courts, it is mandatory to comply with a previous conciliation hearing at the mediation and conciliation office. The mediation and conciliation office is an administrative agency existing in each Autonomous Community.

This hearing gives the parties the opportunity to reach an agreement and avoid excessive litigation. It is not mandatory to be represented by a lawyer, but often, both parties are assisted by one. It is a very quick, informal procedure with no witnesses or evidence at all. The parties appear before a conciliator, who will require them to identify themselves and ask them if there is an agreement. If there is one, the conciliator will put the terms of the agreement in writing. These agreements have the same validity and can be executed as court judgments.

If an agreement is not reached, the claimant may file a claim before the labour court.

25.3. Arbitration

Employees and employers can expressly agree to submit their conflicts to arbitration. The arbiter's decisions have the same validity as judgments.

Certain collective conflicts are subject to arbitration, such as those derived from the interpretation of a collective bargaining agreement or those derived from the election of workers' representatives.

Autonomous Communities have their services of mediation and conciliation, with experts on employment law designed as arbiters.

25.4. Litigation

Once the mandatory mediation and conciliation attempt has been complied with, without reaching an agreement, the claimant may file a claim before the labour courts.

In the case of claims that affect the general interest of a group, derived from the interpretation of a law, collective agreement, or corporate practice, it is possible to file a multi-plaintiff or collective claim. Such claims must be filed by specific parties such as trade unions and company associations or the employer or the employees' legal representation and will be dealt with as an urgent procedure, and it will have preference over other procedures.

25.5. Fines, Penalties and Damages

- The labour administration imposes fines for infringement of labour regulations. Labour fines may range from EUR 70 to EUR 225,018, depending on the seriousness of the infringement. In the case of infringing health and safety at work regulations, fines may be as high as EUR 983,736.
- Infringement of temporary hiring is fined with amounts ranging from EUR 1,000 to EUR 10,000 per affected employee.
- Employers may be subject to additional penalties. Specifically, in the case of industrial accidents, employers can be liable for surcharges on social security pensions. The employer may have to pay the employee (or their relatives) 30% to 50% of the pension to be received by the employee or the beneficiaries of the pension.
- Finally, employers can also be liable for damages (moral or psychological) under Spanish labour law, although it may be necessary to prove and quantify not only the infringement but also the damages derived from the infringement.

25.6. Checklist of Do's and Don'ts

- It is advisable to have legal counsel in any dispute that may affect the company.
- The negotiation process prior to trial is very important, and the parties must approach it with the serious intention of reaching an agreement.

26. EMPLOYER RECORDKEEPING: DATA PROTECTION AND EMPLOYEE ACCESS TO PERSONNEL FILES AND RECORDS

26.1. Overview

Section 18.4 of the Spanish Constitution establishes that 'the law shall limit the use of computer and information technology to guarantee the honour and personal and family intimacy of citizens and the full use of their rights'. The GDPR and the LOPDGDD establish the rules for safeguarding and protecting personal data and civil rights.

This regulation imposes a general obligation to obtain an individual's consent to handle their personal data.

The general principles set forth in the legislation for the Protection of Personal Data in order to guarantee that protection is the following:

- *Principle of purpose limitation*: Employee's personal data may only be collected and used for a certain purpose or reason, which must be specific and legitimate and not processed in a manner that is incompatible with those purposes. For example, data can be collected for recruitment, working schedules management, training, health and safety. An employer cannot create data banks for uncertain reasons.
- *Principle of data minimization*: the data collected must be necessary only for the purposes for which it is being processed. The employer will expressly collect personal data for specific purposes, and the processing of the data must be limited to such purposes.
- *Principle of lawfulness, fairness and transparency*: It is forbidden to obtain data through means that are fraudulent, disloyal, or illicit. For example, employers cannot conduct private investigations of employees or hide the real purpose of the data collection.
- *Principle of accuracy*: The personal data collected must be true, precise and complete. The employer is also obliged to keep the data updated, as well as being responsible for cancellation and/or substitution of data.
- *Storage limitation*: the data must be kept only during the time necessary to execute the purposes for which the data is being processed.
- *Integrity and confidentiality*: the personal data must be granted adequate security measures that ensure its protection against unauthorized processing, loss or damage.
- *Accountability*: the employer will be responsible for compliance with the data protection regulation and must be able to demonstrate such compliance.

The data protection will be by design and by default; therefore, the employer will have an obligation to take all technical and organizational measures to ensure the effective implementation of the aforementioned data protection principles and to integrate the necessary safeguards into the processing. These obligations apply both at the processing of the data and at the time of the determination of the means for processing.

Consent is not required to collect data necessary for the maintenance or compliance of a labour relationship, but the data can only be used for the processing strictly necessary to execute the labour relationship.

However, even if the consent of employees is not required in order to collect and treat their personal data, it is compulsory to inform employees at the time of collection of the data:

- of the existence of the data file, of their ability to use access rights;
- of rights of rectification, erasure, cancellation and opposition;
- the identity and address of the person responsible for the treatment of the data;
- the right to restriction of processing; and

– the right to data portability.

If the data is not collected from the employee but from 'parallel sources', the employer will have to comply with these rights within one month (according to the GDPR) of the registration of the data in the employer's files.

The employer, as the data controller, will have an obligation to be proactive in compliance with the data protection regulation. The main obligations that it must comply with are:

- where applicable, the designation of a Data Protection Officer, in charge of managing the data protection actions carried out by the employer;
- maintain a record of data processing activities that will be available for the authorities;
- notify the data breaches to the competent authorities within a maximum of seventy-two hours since the contingency;
- where applicable, defining the procedures of impact assessment of the data processing that imply high risk, as well as making a prior consultation to the competent authority.

26.2. Confidentiality Rules

The person responsible for the files and any other person taking part in the data management process are bound by professional confidentiality and will continue to be so even when their relationship with the data holder is terminated.

26.3. Checklist of Do's and Don'ts

- Ensure that the personal data processed is accurate, relevant and not excessive in relation to the company's needs.
- Be transparent with regard to who collects the data, how it is processed and how it is being used.
- Do not process employee's sensitive personal data unless the company has a lawful basis for doing so.
- Be vigilant if you are transferring personal data to third parties (it may be necessary to sign a data processor agreement).
- Ensure that all personal data is kept secure, in particular, from unauthorized access.

27. REQUIRED NOTICES AND POSTINGS

27.1. Overview

To give sufficient publicity to certain issues within the company, there must be a notice board in a visible and accessible place. Although this obligation is not expressly established anywhere, it may be inferred from the Workers' Statute, which requires the employer to post certain items on the notice board. Specifically, the employer has an obligation to post the working calendar with all public holidays, the vacation schedule, and the list of voters for the workers' representatives' election.

In addition, section 81, the Workers' Statute, establishes that workers' representatives are entitled to a notice board on which to post the information they may deem interesting for employees. This notice board must be placed in a visible and accessible location within the company.

The evolution of technology has made it possible for these notice boards to be offered online, either on the company's intranet or on the trade union's own webpage.

It is not required to have a notice board for each of the trade unions with representatives within the company; the legal minimum is a 'notice board'.

The omission to provide a notice board for the workers' representatives in a visible and accessible place is a serious infraction with a fine between EUR 751 and EUR 7,500.

27.2. Checklist of Do's and Don'ts

– Avoid interfering with the postings on the workers' representatives' notice board, regardless of the contents of the posting, as such may be considered an attack on the freedom of the representatives.

www.ingramcontent.com/pod-product-compliance
Lightning Source LLC
LaVergne TN
LVHW021112300926
849160LV00009B/708